NOW YOU KNOW

Royalty

NOW YOU KNOW

Royalty

Doug Lennox

DUNDURN PRESS
TORONTO

Editors: Arthur Bousfield and Garry Toffoli
Copy Editor: Allison Hirst
Design: Courtney Horner
Printer: Webcom

Library and Archives Canada Cataloguing in Publication

Lennox, Doug
  Now you know royalty / by Doug Lennox.

ISBN 978-1-55488-415-5

  1. Kings and rulers--Miscellanea. I. Title.

D107.L45 2009   305.5'22   C2009-900498-4

1   2   3   4   5   13   12   11   10   09

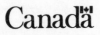 

We acknowledge the support of **The Canada Council for the Arts** and the **Ontario Arts Council** for our publishing program. We also acknowledge the financial support of the **Government of Canada** through the **Book Publishing Industry Development Program** and **The Association for the Export of Canadian Books,** and the **Government of Ontario** through the **Ontario Book Publishers Tax Credit program,** and the **Ontario Media Development Corporation.**

Care has been taken to trace the ownership of copyright material used in this book. The author and the publisher welcome any information enabling them to rectify any references or credits in subsequent editions.

J. Kirk Howard, President

www.dundurn.com

Dundurn Press	Gazelle Book Services Limited	Dundurn Press
3 Church Street, Suite 500	White Cross Mills	2250 Military Road
Toronto, Ontario, Canada	High Town, Lancaster, England	Tonawanda, NY
M5E 1M2	LA1 4XS	U.S.A. 14150

contents

preface

The essence of monarchy is that the state is embodied in a living person and that the monarch's subjects are "people" rather than "the people." This common humanity, celebrated over generations, perhaps accounts for the fascination of most individuals with royal lives and practices. They recognize instinctively that their lives are intimately connected with the lives of the royals. As has been noted, royal activities are frequently ordinary activities carried out in extraordinary circumstances.

From the philosophical underpinnings of the very nature of society, through leadership in times of crisis and adversity, to the great pageantry of communities and the customs of day-to-day living, we function, often unknowingly, in a royal world. Monarchy has been a universal experience. While focusing on Canadian and Commonwealth history and practice, this exploration of royalty considers examples from cultures around the world.

Now You Know Royalty looks at the influence of kings and kingship, the language of monarchy, how monarchies function, the cultural role of kingship, the royal beginnings of everyday practices, and anecdotes involving emperors and empresses, kings and queens, princes and princesses, in the hope that it will both inform and entertain readers. In particular, it seeks to make Canadians aware of their royal heritage and the role that the Crown has played in the creation and history of their country.

the nature
of monarchy

Kingship? Queenship? What is it?

Not an ideology. Not a philosophy. It is more a directing or organizing principle. *Rex*, the Latin word for king, comes from the verb "to direct." A king is someone who sets things in motion, in a constitutional sense, and in past ages in a political one. He is the legal embodiment of a nation or head of a state or multinational family of states. "A king involves an ideal of life at once social and personal."

When did kingship/queenship begin?

The idea began with civilization itself. The earliest kings appear about the same time fundamentals of civilization do. "Royalties found they were representatives almost without knowing. Many a king insisting on a genealogical tree, or a title deed, found that he spoke for the forests and the songs of a whole countryside." Monarchy has been a major force in making civilization possible, causing its development and growth.

Where does the concept that "divinity doth hedge a king" originate?

The earliest kings were seen as having a close relationship with divinity. Some were regarded as living gods, others as kin of the gods, still others as semi-divine. Many kings ritually impersonated or were agents of a god or goddess, executing the deity's will, or priests — those who offer sacrifice — of a divinity. Just as the concepts of morality and law come to us from religion, so do abstract ideas of authority and beliefs about the source of power. Anointing — an act to separate the king from the profane and obtain for him an infusion of divine grace — in later times came to be regarded as giving a sacred sanction to a monarch and bestowing a special character on him.

Quickies

Did you know ...

• that early kings who grew old were sacrificed in a re-creation ritual to assure the continuing vitality of the community?

This semi-sacramental character was thought to make the king a means of healing and led to practices such as "touching for the King's Evil" (scrofula), a type of faith healing. Charles II, it is estimated, touched over 100,000 people. Today this royal quality is attested by the desire of people to touch Queen Elizabeth II.

What kinds of monarchy are there?

There are hereditary, elective, dual, theocratic, absolute, and constitutional monarchies— just about as many types as there have been societies to be governed. Sovereignties have been called empires, kingdoms, dominions, realms, principalities, grand duchies, counties, and commonwealths.

What is hereditary monarchy?

When the crown, on the death of a sovereign, passes automatically from one monarch to another in the same family it is known as a hereditary monarchy. In monarchies such as Britain/the Commonwealth, Denmark, and Japan, the succession has gone on without legal interruption for more than a thousand years.

What is an elective monarchy?

In an elective monarchy the king is chosen, usually for life, by vote. Earliest elected kings were selected — mostly by battle! — from members of the extended royal family. Poland is a state that turned from a hereditary

Order of Succession to Queen Elizabeth II (first 12)

- The Prince Charles, Prince of Wales
- Prince William of Wales
- Prince Harry of Wales
- The Prince Andrew, Duke of York
- Princess Beatrice of York
- Princess Eugenie of York
- The Prince Edward, Earl of Wessex
- James, Viscount Severn [Prince James of Wessex]
- Lady Louise Wessex [Princess Louise of Wessex]
- The Princess Anne, Princess Royal
- Peter Phillips
- Zara Phillips

monarchy into an elective one in 1572. Its kings were chosen by the *szlacta* or landed gentry. But elective monarchy so weakened the Polish kingdom that it ended up being partitioned by its neighbours and disappeared as a state for over a century.

Malaysia, a Commonwealth country, and the papacy are modern elective monarchies. Nine local hereditary sultans in Malaysia meet every five years to choose one amongst them to be king (*Yang di-Pertuan Agong*). The pope is elected, customarily from among the cardinals of the Church, for life. Given its great longevity of nearly 2,000 years, the papacy is the most successful elective monarchy in history. Because it is impossible for the papacy to compromise its spiritual claims, bad or incompetent popes never do irreparable damage to it.

The Dalai Lama, former ruler of Tibet, another elective theocratic monarchy, was chosen by reincarnation. A young child believed to possess the soul of the deceased Dalai Lama was searched for and when discovered was enthroned as the new monarch.

How do absolute, authoritarian, and legislatively responsible monarchies differ?

In an absolute monarchy there is no restraint on the will of the ruler. In authoritarian and legislatively responsible monarchies there are religious, customary, and legal restrictions. In a legislatively responsible monarchy the king or his ministers are, in addition, restrained by a popularly elected body. Edward I expressed the principle underlying the latter: "What touches all," he said, "should be approved by all."

Have there been any absolute regimes in modern times?

There have been no absolute monarchies in modern times, but there have been many absolute republics. Lenin and Stalin's Soviet Union, Hitler's Germany, Mao's China, and Pol Pot's Cambodia are examples.

Monarchs Who Changed History	
Cyrus "the Great"	Persia
Darius I "the Great"	Persia
Chandragupta Maurya	India
Alexander III "the Great"	Greece, Asia Minor, Persia, Egypt
Constantine I "the Great"	Roman Empire, East and West
Tiridates IV "the Great"	Armenia
Clovis I	France
Charlemagne	France, Germany, Italy
Arpad	Hungary
Rurik	Russia
Alexius I Comnenus	Byzantium
Ivan Asen II	Bulgaria, Thrace, Albania, Greece, Macedonia
Uroš Stephen "the Great"	DusănSerbia
William "the Conqueror"	England
Alfonso I Henriques	Portugal
Robert "the Bruce"	Scotland
St. Vladimir I	Russia
Pachacutec Inca Yupanquil	Ecuador, Peru, Chile
Mohammed II	Turkey, Balkans, Mediterranean
Montezuma II	Mexico
Jan III Sobieski	Western Europe
Peter "the Great"	Russia
Napoleon I	France, Europe, United States
Victor Emmanuel II	Italy

What is the difference between an authoritarian monarch and a tyrant?

The clever though often pedantic King James I and VI explained the difference in his first speech to the English Parliament on inheriting the crowns of England and Ireland in 1603. "The special and greatest point of difference that is between a rightful king and an usurping tyrant is this: That whereas the proud and ambitious tyrant doth think his kingdoms and people are only ordained for the satisfaction of his desires and unreasonable appetites, the righteous and just king doth by the contrary acknowledge himself to be ordained for the procuring of the wealth and property of his people," His Majesty said.

Subjects of which sovereign prince recently voted to retain authoritarian monarchy?

Karl Adam, Prince of Liechtenstein. In a democratic referendum held in 2003, the people of Liechtenstein chose overwhelmingly to keep the form of government in which the prince is sovereign. The principality's government, nonetheless, operates day by day in approved democratic fashion.

How does royal sovereignty contrast with republican sovereignty?

In a republic, sovereignty is usually vested in "the people," a theoretical concept. In a monarchy, sovereignty is vested in a real person.

How does a monarchy differ from a republic?

Under a monarchy, society is seen as an extended family. "Royalty," a scholar has written, "forms the nuclear family of the whole nation — or even, by inter-marriage, the nuclear family that binds nations together." Or, as Vincent Massey put it in his Coronation Day broadcast: "The queen is the head of our nation, and our nation, as we contemplate her headship, becomes a household itself." Contrariwise republics see society only as a public corporation.

How does monarchy work?

In a constitutional parliamentary monarchy such as Canada, the underlying structure of the law and its imagery are that the queen/king is doing everything in person. The Crown's function is to set the entire apparatus of government in motion. The queen creates a government, summons, prorogues and dissolves Parliament, issues election writs, sends bills to Parliament to be made into laws, proclaims laws once passed, administers the laws, provides judges and civil servants to carry out her commands through her government, makes treaties, and sends her armed forces into action.

All such queenly acts are done by and on the advice of ministers (*minister* means "servant") who, as members of the committee of her Privy Council called the cabinet, are her only legal advisers, and are drawn from members of Parliament who enjoy the confidence (i.e. can command the majority support) of the House of Commons.

At the same time this works democratically, with ultimate responsibility for giving the sovereign her advisers lying with the electorate. It is a marriage of two principles: royal authority and democratic control. If royal authority and its imagery are forgotten, however, the other parts of the system lose their meaning. That is why in recent times MPs who do not understand the Crown have interrupted the Speech from the Throne

Quickies

Did you know …

- that the coronation is a symbolic bringing together of every role of kingship: acclamation, oath to govern justly and defend the people, ritual death and rebirth through anointing, robing in special clothes, crowning, enthronement, and "homage from great of the land"?

Louis XIV's Maxims on Kingship

- "The function of kings consists mainly in letting good sense take its course."
- "A king should listen rather than speak, because it is difficult to say much without saying too much."
- "Every time I make an appointment, I make one ungrateful person and a hundred with a grievance."
- "It seems to me that we [kings] must be at the same time humble on our own account, and proud on account of the office we fill."
- "A man reigns by work and it is ungrateful and presumptuous to God, unjust and tyrannical to men, to wish to reign without working."

with applause or jeers and why people talk about electing a government instead of electing a Parliament.

Who originated our system of justice available to all?

This cornerstone of our modern society comes directly from King Henry II, the monarch who ruled the Angevin Empire, consisting of England and the greater part of France, from 1154 to 1189. A fully literate ruler, fluent in French and English and with a good knowledge of Latin, Henry II came to the throne after a period of bitter civil war, during which law and order had completely broken down. The king ordered his chancery to begin issuing writs that ran in his name, allowing any freeman in the kingdom to obtain a remedy in the local court, or if that failed, in the king's court. To make sure that his justice was readily accessible, the king also sent out judges who made regular journeys around the kingdom. About the year 1180, he set up a Royal Court at Westminster, which sat permanently. With the decline and disappearance of serfdom in the succeeding centuries, "freeman" came to include everyone in the kingdom.

Quickies

Did you know ...

- that as fount of justice, the queen is seen to be so dedicated to her people's welfare that she is presumed by law never to condone wrongdoing?

What is "loyal opposition"?

A concept developed under constitutional monarchy. It means that if you do it peacefully and lawfully, you can oppose the measures of the government of the day without being regarded as disloyal. The Criminal Code of Canada states: "No person shall be deemed to have a seditious

Quickies

Did you know ...

- that the royal prerogative is power that belongs to the queen simply in right of being sovereign and is not conferred on her by statute of Parliament? "Reason to rule, but mercy to forgive: The first is law, the last is prerogative."

Regal Remarks

- Henry II, about his ex-Chancellor, Thomas Becket: "Who will free me from this turbulent priest?"
- Rudolf I, on his approachability: "I have not become King to live in a closet."
- Edward III, about his son, the Black Prince at Crécy: "Let the boy win his spurs!"
- Louis XII, who before ascending the throne was Duke of Orleans: "The King of France does not avenge injuries done to the Duke of Orleans."
- Sigismund: "I am the Emperor Sigismund and above the rules of grammar."
- Frederick III: "The House of Austria is destined to rule the world."
- Maximilian I: "If only we had peace we'd be sitting in a rose garden."
- Charles V, on Martin Luther: "A single friar who goes contrary to all Christianity for a thousand years must be wrong."
- Mary I: "When I am dead and opened, you shall find 'Calais' lying in my heart."
- Elizabeth I, in her Golden Speech to Parliament: "Though God hath raised me high, yet this I count the glory of my crown: that I have reigned with your loves."
- Philip II, on the defeat of his great armada: "I sent my ships against men, not against waves."
- James I: "No bishop, no king."
- Ferdinand I: "Let justice be done, though the world perish."
- Charles I: "I am the martyr of the people."
- Louis XIV, when his grandson became king of Spain: "The Pyrenees have ceased to exist."
- Peter I "the Great": "I hope God will forgive me my many sins because of the good I have tried to do for my people."
- Louis XV: "After me the flood!"
- Francis I, to the child Mozart: "You are a little sorcerer!"
- Napoleon I: "There is only one step from the sublime to the ridiculous."
- Nicholas II: "I do not wish for war; as a rule I shall do all in my power to preserve for my people the benefits of peace."
- Shah Mohammad Reza Pahlavi, when compared to the "democratic" king of Sweden: "I could govern like the king of Sweden if my people were like the Swedish people."

intention by reason only that he intends … to show that Her Majesty has been misled and mistaken in her measures."

How international has monarchy been?

So international that it has bridged geography, race, and religion. Here is an example: Henry III, King of England, married Eleanor of Provence.

One of Eleanor's sisters was married to St. Louis IX, King of France, and yet another, Beatrix, to King Charles I of Naples. Charles and Beatrix's son, Charles II, King of Naples, married Mary, daughter of Stephen V, King of Hungary. King Charles II's wife's sister, Anna, married Andronicus II Paleologus, Emperor of Byzantium. Andronicus' half sister, Maria, married Abaqa, Il-khan of Persia, whose uncle was Kublai Khan, Emperor of China. A few simple royal and imperial relationships and connections covering about 40 years connected Henry III of England with the Emperor of China, neither of whom was even aware of the other's existence.

Which kings and queens were the only ones anointed with pure chrism?

The monarchs of England and France. Chrism is a combination of olive oil and balsam blessed on Maundy Thursday. Other monarchs were anointed with simple olive oil.

Who has a right to a bow or curtsy?

All monarchs, Imperial and Royal Highnesses, members of sovereign or former sovereign families with the titles of Serene Highness and up. Governors general and spouses as personal representatives of a monarch are also entitled to a bow or curtsy but not lieutenant-governors who represent the sovereign at a remove.

For what maxim is the sagacious Louis XVIII best known?

Arriving on the hour for a council meeting, the king's ministers found Louis XVIII already sitting at the head of the table awaiting them. To their apologies for having kept him waiting and compliments on his being ahead of time, His Majesty replied: "Punctuality is the politeness of kings."

How does monarchy favour multicultural societies?

In a monarchy, unity is defined through personal allegiance to the sovereign of the country or empire rather than adherence to an ideology, membership in a racial or ethnic group, or commitment to an historical revolution or event. As the Canadian historian W.L. Morton wrote, "Any one, French, Irish, Ukrainian, or Inuit, can be a subject of the Queen and a citizen of Canada without in any way changing or ceasing to be himself." In his accession speech to the Cortés, King Juan Carlos I of Spain said: "The King wishes to be at once the King of all and the King of each one in his own culture, history and tradition."

What are the rights of a king or queen in a constitutional monarchy?

Most monarchies, especially those in the British tradition, do not have specifically defined rights. The great constitutional writer Walter Bagehot

Monarchs Who United Peoples	
Menes	Upper Egypt and Lower Egypt
Edgar "the Peaceable"	English, Danes, Welsh, and Scots
Kenneth I MacAlpine	Picts and Scots
Canute	Danes, Norwegians, Swedes, and Saxons
Eric IV	Swedes and Goths
Margaret	Danes, Norwegians, and Swedes
Ferdinand and Isabella	Castillians and Aragonese
Ferdinand I	Germans, Czechs, and Hungarians
Henri IV	French and Navarese
James I	English, Scots, and Irish
Leopold I	Flemish and Walloons
Wladislow II Jagiello	Poles and Lithuanians
Peter II	Serbs, Croats, Slovenians, Montenegrans

suggested, however, that the rights could be best described as the right to be consulted, the right to encourage, and the right to warn.

What is the Civil List?

The Civil List is income derived from the revenue of the Crown Estates (land owned by the sovereign in right of the United Kingdom) and set aside to cover the public expenses of the Crown. The Civil List began in 1689 and originally covered the cost of the armed forces and the expenses of civil government paid by the hereditary revenue of the Crown and by some taxes. In 1760, King George III turned over the entire hereditary revenue to Parliament, which then assumed the full cost of government and paid an allowance to the monarch for specifically royal expenses. At the beginning of each reign this arrangement is renewed.

What is the Act of Settlement?

The Act of Settlement, passed in 1701, governs the succession to the throne in Commonwealth countries and requires, among other things, that the monarch be in communion with the Church of England, and not be, nor be married to, a Catholic. It was passed in the reign of King William III, who had no children, to ensure that after his sister-in-law Anne, who was next in line to the throne, the crown would not pass to the Catholic descendants of his father-in-law, King James II, whom he had overthrown in 1689. Through the principle of "received law," the act is part of the constitutional law of Canada and can only be altered by an amendment unanimously approved by the Senate, House of Commons, and provincial legislative assemblies.

What does the Royal Marriages Act require?

The Royal Marriages Act, passed in 1772, requires members of the British royal family to obtain the consent of the sovereign to their marriage prior to the age of 25. They may then marry without consent if Parliament does not object within 12 months. The act was passed at the request of King George III to allow him to control the marital choices of his sons after some unsuitable alliances had been made by members of the royal family.

Where does sovereignty lie in Canada?

Canadian sovereignty is vested in the reigning monarch (currently Queen Elizabeth II). The Constitution Act, 1867, states clearly: "The executive government and authority of and over Canada is hereby declared to continue and be vested in the Queen."

Has monarchy affected Canada?

It's no exaggeration to say that without monarchy there would have been no Canada. As well as the role monarchs generally played in its exploration and settlement, specific actions of monarchs were crucial to its creation. Had Louis XIV not made Quebec a royal province, French Canada would not have survived. If the Loyalists had not loved their king and constitution, Canada today would be the northern extension of the United States. When the American Revolution ended, George III told those negotiating the peace that he would never agree to abandon Canada, the West Indies, and Newfoundland. Sure enough, the victorious Americans arrived at the peace talks demanding all of North America. They did not get it. In 1867, only the deep loyalty felt to Queen Victoria allowed the provinces of Canada to overcome their rivalries, narrow sectionalism, and unite.

How did the Fathers of Confederation view The Crown?

The Fathers of Confederation were unanimous in supporting the monarchical form of government for the new country. Sir George Étienne Cartier called the monarchy the "essential element" of the constitution.

People on Kingship

"The King's name is a tower of strength." — *Richard III*, V.iii, Shakespeare

'Tis a duteous thing
To show all honour to an earthly king." — Anonymous

"Kings will be tyrants from policy, when subjects are rebels from principle." — *Reflections on the French Revolution*, Burke

"The King never dies." — Blackstone, book 1.17

"Is it not passing brave to be a king
And ride in triumph through Persepolis?" — *Conquests of Tamburlaine*, Marlowe, book 1

"Where the word of a king is, there is power." — Ecclesiastes, 8.4, the Bible

"A substitute shines brightly as a king
Until a King be by." — *Merchant of Venice*, act 5, scene 1, Shakespeare

"The King must not be under man but under God and under the law, because the law makes the King." — Bracton

"Honour all men. Love the brotherhood. Fear God. Honour the King." — Epistle of St. James, 1.17, the Bible

"The King is the centre of the majesty of the whole community." — Blackstone

"I found that monarchy was the best government for the poor to live in, and commonwealths for the rich." — *The Vicar of Wakefield*, Goldsmith

"Not all the water in the rough rude sea
Can wash the balm from an anointed king;
The breath of worldly men cannot depose
The deputy elected by the Lord." — *Richard II*, act 3, scene 2, Shakespeare

"'Twixt kings and tyrants there's this difference known;
Kings seek their subjects' good; tyrants their own." — *Kings and Tyrants*, Herrick

"Ultimately, mercy is the surest sign by which the world may distinguish a true king." — Corneille

"The Queen's government must be carried on." — Duke of Wellington

"What is a King — a man condemn'd to bear
The public burden of the nation's care." — *Solomon*, book 3, Prior

"Who made thee a prince and a judge over us?" — Exodus, 2.14, the Bible

"Live pure, speak true, right wrong, follow the King —
Else, wherefore born?" — *Gareth and Lynette*, 1.117, Tennyson

"The mind is free, whate'er afflict the man,
A King's a King, do fortune what she can." — *The Barrons' Wars*, Michael Drayton

"There is only one species of interest felt for dethroned monarchs — how they bear their misfortunes." — Charles Lever

"There's such divinity doth hedge a King,
That treason can but peep to what it would." — *Hamlet*, act 4, scene 5, Shakespeare

"I believe that constitutional monarchy is the best defence of democracy." — Yehudi Menuhin

In the Confederation Debates it was resolved that the government of the new country would be carried on "by the Sovereign in person or by her representative duly authorized."

What does the inscription on the Peace Tower in Ottawa mean?

The motto of the Royal Arms of Canada, *A mari usque ad mare* ("From sea to sea") is taken from the 72nd Psalm — "And he [the King] shall have dominion from sea to sea and from the river unto the ends of the earth." It is this psalm from which the name "Dominion of Canada" is also drawn. The beginning of the psalm is "Give the King thy judgments, O God, and thy righteousness unto the King's son." The cornerstone of the Peace Tower was laid in 1919 by Prince Edward, Prince of Wales, the son of King George V, and it is the first part of the 72nd Psalm that is carved on the Peace Tower.

Philosophers of Kingship

Plato	"The Philosopher as King," Books V to VII of *The Republic* (Athens, fourth century B.C.)
Aristotle	*Politics* (Greece, fourth century B.C.)
Henry de Bracton	*Treatise on the Laws of England* (England, before 1268)
St. Thomas Aquinas	*On Kingship, To The King Of Cyprus* (Italy, before 1274)
Niccolò Machiavelli	*The Prince* (Florence, 1514)
Claude de Seyssel	*La Grant Monarchie de France* (Turin, 1519)
Sir John Fortescue	*In Praise of the Laws of England* and *Monarchia*
John Aylmer	*An Harborowe for Faithfull* and *Trewe Subjects*
James I	*Trew Law of Free Monarchies* (Scotland, 1598)
Thomas Hobbes	*Leviathan* (England, 1651)
François de La Mothe-Fénelon	*Les Aventures de Télémaque* and *Table de Chaulnes*
Sir Robert Filmer	*Patriarcha* (England, 1680)
John Locke	*Treatises of Government* (England, 1690)
Henry St. John, Viscount Bolingbroke	*The Idea of a Patriot King* (Britain, 1738)
Charles de Secondat, Baron de Montesquieu	*Spirit of the Laws* (France, 1748)
Edmund Burke	*Reflections on the French Revolution* (Britain, 1790)
Louis, Viscount de Bonald	*Theory of Political and Religious Power in Civil Society* (France, 1796)
Joseph, Count de Miastre	*Essay on the Generating Principle of Political Constitutions* (Sardinia, 1810)
Walter Bagehot	*The English Constitution* (British Empire, 1867)
John Farthing	*Freedom Wears a Crown* (Canada, 1957)

royal
nomenclature

What is the difference between the terms *imperial* and *royal*?

Though the word *royal* is often used to refer to all monarchs, it correctly only refers to a monarch of a kingdom and his or her family. Thus an empire has an imperial family (Japan), a kingdom (or dominion) has a royal family (United Kingdom, Canada), and a principality has a princely family (Monaco).

Quickies

Did you know ...

- that *dominion* and *realm* are synonyms for *kingdom*?

Where did the rulers of China and Japan get the title *Emperor*?

The title was adopted from the West. It was the descriptive term applied to them by Europeans and, in that sense, it, too comes from the Roman Empire. The Chinese and Japanese themselves had a quite different name for their rulers — the "Son of Heaven."

Quickies

Did you know ...

- that *Caesar* (Julius Caesar and Augustus Caesar) is the root for the titles *tsar* (Russia), *kaiser* (Germany), and *shah* (Iran)?

What was the first imperial dynasty of China?

The short-lived Ch'in dynasty, whose ruler, Shih Huang-Ti, was the first emperor. The dynasty gave its name to China.

Which king was styled Emperor of Britain?

King Edgar, one of the Saxon monarchs. *Empire* does not inherently mean a geographically large entity as it is used in popular parlance. It means independent of any other sovereignty. "This England is an Empire," declared Henry VIII by statute. Kings were originally subordinate to emperors.

Was the British monarch ever Emperor or Empress of the British Empire?

Although there was a British Empire, there has not been a "British Emperor" or "Empress" since 1066, and the title has remained King or Queen. Queen Victoria was proclaimed Empress of India, though, in 1877, and the title Emperor of India was borne by the next four monarchs — Edward VII, George V, Edward VIII, and George VI. India became a dominion under King George VI, and a republic before Elizabeth II came to the throne, so George VI was the last Emperor of India.

What does the word *king* mean?

King comes from the Old English word *cyning*. It means "scion of the kin" or "son of the kindred," the kindred being sacral royalty who were seen as the kin of the gods. *Cyning* is connected with the Old Norse word *konungr*, a combination of *kin* and *ung* meaning "descendant." The German word for king — *könig* — is also related and the Russian word for prince — *kniaz* — derives from *konungr* too. Everyone knows that the Latin word for king is *rex*. From the same root come other forms of the name: the Irish *ri* (*ard-ri* is "high king"), Hindu *raja* (*maharaja* means "great king"), French *roi*, Italia *re*, Spanish *rey*, and so on. Kingship is a world-wide phenomenon.

What does *queen* mean?

Queen can have two meanings. A "queen regnant" is a reigning monarch in her own right. A "queen consort" is the wife of a reigning king. In many European countries women could not reign, and in those where they now can, it took centuries for women to establish their right to do so.

Ranks in British/Commonwealth Peerage

- Duke/Duchess
- Marquess/Marchioness
- Earl/Countess
- Viscount/Viscountess
- Baron/Baroness

Who was the first English monarch officially addressed as Your Majesty?

King Henry VIII was the first to be so addressed. Prior to him, the monarchs were addressed as Your Grace, and Your Majesty was reserved for the emperor. Henry VIII asserted that England was subordinate to no other authority than himself so that it was an empire in law, although the title itself was not adopted.

How did the term *Britannic Majesty* originate?

It came out of the Jacobite Court of the exiled King James II at St. Germaine-en-Laye. Accustomed to hearing their host, King Louis XIV, referred to as "His Most Christian Majesty," the Jacobites took to calling their master "His Britannic Majesty." When it became known, the term was borrowed by the Hanoverian kings of the British Empire and became official.

What is a pretender?

The term *pretender* is incorrectly used to describe a former monarch or descendant of a dethroned house who seeks to be restored to the Crown. The proper term for such a person, however, is *claimant*, not *pretender*. The individual is asserting old rights, not making a pretense of something to which he is not entitled. Pretender is rightly applied to people such as Perkin Warbeck or the False Dimitry who were imposters. Misuse of the word *pretender* comes from its application to the exiled Stuart claimants, James III, Charles III, and Henry IX. The ambiguity attached to it led John Byrom to write his doggerel:

> God bless the King! — I mean the Faith's Defender,
> God bless (no harm in blessing) the Pretender!
> But who Pretender is, or who is King,
> God bless us all! — that's quite another thing.

Who is the King or Queen of England?

Nobody! Though beloved of the media, the title has not existed since 1707. Queen Anne (1701–1714) was the last Queen of England. With the union of England and Scotland, the titles King of England and King of Scotland disappeared. From then on the monarch was King or Queen of Great Britain. Elizabeth II is Queen of the United Kingdom of Great Britain and Northern Ireland, Queen of Canada, Queen of Jamaica, etc., but not Queen of England. England, of course, is part of her realm of Great Britain and Northern Ireland.

Some monarchs have been called "the Great." What are some sobriquets that have been given to others?

Many rulers have been given names denoting their physical characteristics, character traits (good and bad), and record as rulers. Here are some examples:

- William "the Conqueror" (England)
- Baldwin IV "the Leper" (Jerusalem)
- Charles II "the Merry Monarch" (Britain/Commonwealth)
- Iorweth "Flat-Nosed" (Wales)
- William "the Silent" (Netherlands)
- Robert "the Devil" (Normandy)
- Leo VI "the Philosopher" (Byzantium)
- Eochaid "the Venomous" (Scotland)
- Aedh "the Lazy-Arsed Youth" (Ireland)
- Maximilian I "the last of the Knights" (Holy Roman Empire)
- Juana "the Mad" (Spain)
- Abdul "the Damned" (Ottoman Empire)
- Ivan "the Dread" (Russia)
- Albert II "the Degenerate" (Germany)
- Magnus VI "Law Mender" (Denmark)
- Frederick "the Winter King" (Bohemia)

- Mircea III "the Shepherd" (Valachia)
- Alfonso XI "the Avenger" (Castile and Leon)
- Carlos II "the Bewitched" (Spain)
- Edward I "the English Justinian" (England).

What near idolatrous terms were applied to Elizabeth I?

Among them were the Sun Queen, Second Maid, Second Sun, Virgin Queen, Gloriana, Belphoebe, Sweet Cynthia, Deborah, Beauteous Queen of Second Troy, Monarch Maiden Queen, and Astraea.

How many titles did the emperor Charles V possess?

Quickies

Did you know ...

- that the kingdom of Saudi Arabia takes its name from the ruling royal family, the House of Saud?

The emperor had some 75 titles. Some of them were: Holy Roman Emperor, Archduke of Austria, King of Castile and Leon, King of Aragon and Sicily, King of Naples, King of the Romans, Duke of Burgundy, Duke of Brabant, Duke of Limburg, Duke of Lothier, Duke of Luxembourg, Duke of Guelders, Margrave of Namur, Count Palatine of Burgundy, Count of Artois, Count of Charolais, Count of Flanders, Count of Hainault, Count of Holland, Count of Zeeland, and Count of Zutphen.

Why did Maximilian I style himself Emperor Electus?

On election, Holy Roman Emperors were termed *Romanorum rex* — "King of the Romans." Only when crowned by the pope did they become *Romanorum imperator* — "Emperor of the Romans." Maximilian I was unable to get to Rome to be crowned so he obtained from the pope the style *Imperator electus* — "Emperor Elect." It was continued by his successors down to the dissolution of the empire in 1806.

What is the name of the royal family of Thailand?

The Chakri dynasty is the name of the royal family. The present monarch, King Bhumibol Adulyadej Rama IX, is the ninth sovereign of the dynasty.

Pre-British emperors of India were known as Moghul emperors. What does *Moghul* mean?

It is a form of the word *Mongol*. The Indian imperial Timurid dynasty was founded by Tamerlane, who conquered northern India with a Muslim Mongol and Turkish force. One of the army's minor princes, Babur, seized Delhi and created the Moghul Empire in 1526.

How will reigning descendants of Elizabeth II be numbered?

Up till now they have taken the numbering of English sovereigns or used English and Scottish numbers together, i.e. James II and VII. In the future, if there are monarchs with both English and Scottish predecessors of the same name, the higher number of one of the old kingdoms will be used alone. The next King James for example will be James VIII, not III, III and VIII, nor XI (total number of Jameses).

Quickies

Did you know ...

- that the Royal House of Windsor took its name from Windsor Castle in 1917, when it was changed during the First World War from Saxe-Coburg-Gotha, due to anti-German sentiment?

How do the Japanese name the reigns of their monarchs?

Following the death of an emperor, a special name is given to the reign, reflecting the ethos of the time. Emperor Hirohito's reign is known as *Showa*, meaning "Enlightened Peace," to reflect the emperor's opposition

English/British/Commonwealth Dynastic Names (since 1066)	
Norman	1066–1154
Plantagenet	1154–1399
Lancaster	1399–1461
York	1461–1485
Tudor	1485–1603
Stuart and Orange	1603–1714
Brunswick or Hanover	1714–1901
Saxe-Coburg-Gotha	1901–1917
Windsor	1917–present

to his government's policies that brought Japan into the Second World War and his efforts to rebuild a peaceful Japan after its defeat.

Why has the name of the royal family changed from time to time?

The name of the British/Commonwealth royal family has changed when the dynasty changed. The change has occurred for one of three reasons: the reigning branch of the royal family had no direct legitimate successors so a cousin from another branch of the family which had its own name took the throne (e.g. the change from Tudor to Stuart); the reigning branch was overthrown or defeated in war (e.g. York to Tudor, Bourbon to Brunswick in Canada), or a queen regnant married and her son assumed his father's name (e.g. Brunswick to Saxe-Coburg-Gotha). Queen Elizabeth II has decreed her desire that her successors retain the name Windsor. If this is followed then the pattern of changing dynasties would come to an end and all future monarchs would belong to the House of Windsor.

What did the two great British queens, Victoria and Boadicea, have in common?

Boadicea in the ancient British language means the same as "Victoria." She led the Britons in rebellion against their Roman occupiers and is remembered in history as a great patriotic warrior queen.

One of the earliest known legal codes bears a king's name. Who was he?

Hammurabi, King of Babylon, who died in 1750 B.C. The code was carved upon a black stone monument, eight feet high, and was intended to be read by all. The monument is currently on display at the Louvre museum in Paris.

Why are British kings and queens called "Defender of the Faith"?

During the Middle Ages, the king of France became known by the special designation of "His Most Christian Majesty." All the other kings were envious of this and wished special titles for themselves. The king of Portugal became "His Most Faithful Majesty," the king of Hungary "His Apostolic Majesty," and the king of Spain "His Most Catholic Majesty." King Henry VIII was no exception. In 1521, he wrote a book called *Defence of the Seven Sacraments*, which attacked the views of Martin Luther, the Protestant reformer. The king sent the book to the pope, Leo X, who was so pleased with it that he gave the king the title "Defender of the Faith," or in Latin, *Fidei Defensor*, to be borne by Henry and his successors. Although King Henry VIII shortly afterwards broke with the pope, he and the sovereigns after him kept the title. Consequently, Mary I and James II, who were Roman Catholics; Charles I, who was a passionate Anglican; George I, who had been a Lutheran before becoming king;

Canadian Provinces Named After Royalty

- Alberta (Princess Louise Alberta, daughter of Queen Victoria)
- New Brunswick (Royal House of Brunswick)
- Prince Edward Island (Prince Edward, Duke of Kent, father of Queen Victoria)

Australian States Named After Royalty

- Queensland (Queen Victoria)
- Victoria (Queen Victoria)

American States Named After Royalty

- Georgia (King George II)
- Louisiana (King Louis XIV)
- Maryland (Queen Henrietta Maria, wife of King Charles I)
- New York (Prince James, Duke of York, later King James II)
- North Carolina (King Charles I)
- South Carolina (King Charles I)
- Virginia (Queen Elizabeth I — "The Virgin Queen")
- West Virginia (Queen Elizabeth I — "The Virgin Queen")

Quickies

Did you know ...

- that the royal title "Defender of the Faith" harks back to the most ancient days when monarch was both priest and king?

and Queen Victoria, who, although an Anglican, was really more sympathetic to Presbyterianism, were all known as "Defender of the Faith." In 1953, separate styles and titles were adopted by the queen for each of her independent realms on the advice of their respective parliaments. For Canada, the queen retained Defender of the Faith but it was redefined again. The prime minister, Louis St. Laurent, explained in the House of Commons that for Canada, which has no state church, but people "who have faith in the direction of human affairs by an all-wise Providence," the title would henceforth mean "a believer in and a defender of the faith in a supreme ruler."

Which of Canada's monarchs was King of Scots in right of his wife?

King François II of France was married to Mary, Queen of Scots, in 1558 when he was a prince. At his marriage he became King of Scots. In 1559, he succeeded his father as the king of France, but died in 1560.

What is a Crown Victoria?

The Crown Victoria is a full-size automobile made by the Ford Motor Company in St. Thomas, Ontario, and favoured by police forces throughout North America as their standard cruiser. The name originated in a style of carriage designed in France in the 1830s and named after the then Princess Victoria (later Queen Victoria) that featured an elegant low body. The name was eventually passed on to horseless carriages (automobiles) of a similar style.

Quickies

Did you know ...

- that George VI's dramatic and moving broadcast on D-Day calling his people to prayer for victory was an exercise of the monarch's ancient priestly role?

36

Who was the city of New York named after?

Arguably the greatest city in the world, New York was settled by Dutch explorers in 1624 and originally called New Amsterdam. When it was ceded to the British Crown in 1664 it was renamed New York in honour of the brother of King Charles II, Prince James, Duke of York, who later became King James II.

> **Quickies**
> *Did you know ...*
> * that Rotten Row, the famous bridle path for horses in the heart of London, is a corruption of the original French name *Route du Roi* or "King's Way"?

What was the first ship to cross the Atlantic *mostly* under steam?

The *Royal William*, constructed and christened in Quebec City in 1831, with engines built in Montreal, was named in honour of King William IV. In 1833 it sailed from Pictou, Nova Scotia, to Gravesend, England, in 25 days with a crew of 36, seven passengers, and a cargo of coal. Every four days she had to stop and clear her boilers of salt.

> **Quickies**
> *Did you know ...*
> * that Constitution Hill in London is not named to mark a political milestone but because it was the path along which King Charles II took his daily "constitutional" (walk)?

What does the motto of the Prince of Wales, "Ich Dien," mean?

Ich dien is German and means "I serve." It is actually the motto of the heir to the throne, whether or not he, or she, is the Prince of Wales, and was thus the motto of Queen Elizabeth II when she was Princess Elizabeth.

Why does the Prince of Wales sign his name Charles P.?

"Charles P." is short for Charles Princeps. *Princeps* is the Latin word for prince. This is how the heir to the throne has signed his name for hundreds of years. He is the only son of the sovereign who uses the *p*, which he does because he is the Prince of Wales. The word *princeps* is used because Latin was the language of the law and diplomacy when the practice began. In Canada, this princely signature gave rise to the name E.P. Ranch for the High River, Alberta, property owned by Prince Edward, Prince of Wales, later King Edward VIII. The present Prince of Wales signed "Charles P." for the first time when he signed the register for his wedding at St. Paul's Cathedral on July 29, 1981.

Which British dukedoms are held by the heir to the throne?

Upon the accession to the throne of Queen Elizabeth II, Prince Charles automatically became Duke of Cornwall in England and Duke of Rothesay in Scotland.

Incognitos and Aliases of Royalty	
Charles I	Jack Smith
Charles II	William Jackson
Peter "the Great"	Peter Mikhailoff
Anne	Mrs. Morley
(Jacobite) James III	Chevalier de St. George
(Jacobite) Charles III	Betty Burke, Lewie Cawe, James Thompson
Louis XVI	Durand, a steward
Marie Antoinette	Madame Rochet
Louis Philippe	Chabaud de la Tour
Victoria	Lady Churchill, Countess of Balmoral, Countess of Kent
Edward VII	Lord Renfrew

Which king named his eldest son and intended heir Arthur?

Henry VII. Prince Arthur died in his teens. So strong was the influence of the Arthurian legend that speculation is that had the prince succeeded to the throne it would have been as Arthur *the second*.

Who gave the word *Canadian* its modern meaning?

In the days of New France, *Canadien* referred to the ancestors of modern French Canadians. After the Treaty of Paris in 1763 transferred New France to the British Crown, and English and Scottish settlers established themselves, the name continued to refer to those of French descent. The first known use of *Canadian* in its modern civic sense, meaning a resident of Canada regardless of ethnicity, dates from the first election to the Assembly of Lower Canada in 1791. The 23-year-old Prince Edward, son of the king and future father of Queen Victoria, who was then resident in Quebec City, broke up a riot between English and French voters and demanded of them, "Part then in peace. Let me hear no more of the odious distinction of English and French. You are all His Britannic Majesty's beloved Canadian subjects."

What does "True North" mean in the English version of the anthem "O Canada"?

"True North" was borrowed from Alfred, Lord Tennyson's poem in which he refers to Canada as "That True North whereof we lately heard" in reference to its loyalty to Queen Victoria. It does not mean the North Pole or the real north, implying that the northern lands of other countries are false. It is the use of *true* in its other context of meaning loyal or faithful, as, for example, lovers are described as "true to each other." The line of the anthem is describing Canada as loyal to the Crown: "We see thee rise / The True North strong and free."

Quickies

Did you know ...

- that Coronation Gulf in the Northwest Territories was named in honour of George IV's coronation in 1821?

Named After Elizabeth II in Canada

- Queen Elizabeth Hotel, Montreal
- Queen Elizabeth Theatre, Vancouver
- The Queensway, Ottawa
- Place Reine Elizabeth II, Trois-Rivières
- Queen Elizabeth Hospital, Edmonton
- Queen Elizabeth Building, Toronto
- Queen Elizabeth II Park, Windsor
- Queen Elizabeth Island, Northwest Territories
- Queen Elizabeth II Court, Regina
- Queen Elizabeth II Canadian Fund to Aid in Research on the Diseases of Children
- Parc Reine Elizabeth II, La Pocatière
- Queen Elizabeth School, Perth
- Golden Jubilee Park, Haliburton
- Queen Elizabeth Ranges, Alberta
- Queen Elizabeth Planetarium, Edmonton
- Princess Elizabeth Hospital, Winnipeg
- Queen Elizabeth Foreland, Northwest Territories
- Queen Elizabeth II Admission Scholarships
- Queen Elizabeth II Cup for show jumping
- Queen Elizabeth Silver Jubilee Endowment Fund

What Canadian post-nominals does Elizabeth II have the right to?

Her Majesty has the right to the letters U.E., which stand for Unity of the Empire. In 1789, the governor general, Lord Dorchester, decreed that Loyalists from the American Revolution who had "adhered to the unity of the empire and joined the royal standard in America, before the treaty of separation in the year 1783" would be entitled to a "Mark of Honour" and could designate themselves "United Empire Loyalists." Queen Elizabeth II is descended from two Loyalists, one on her mother's side and the other on her father's, and could designate herself "U.E." if she so wished.

> **Quickies**
> *Did you know ...*
> • that Crown Royal whisky was created by Seagram's to mark the 1939 tour of Canada by King George VI and Queen Elizabeth?

> **Quickies**
> *Did you know ...*
> • that Canada is the only country to have two capitals named after Queen Victoria — Victoria, British Columbia, and Regina ("Queen"), Saskatchewan?

What are the words of the Loyal Toast?

The only proper words for the Loyal Toast are "The Queen." Some Canadians like to say "The Queen of Canada" to emphasize the Canadian status of the queen, but correctly one only mentions a country if it is a monarch foreign to the person proposing the toast. Thus, only a foreigner should toast "The Queen of Canada."

What are royal warrant holders?

They are companies that supply goods and services to Queen Elizabeth II, the Duke of Edinburgh, or the Prince of Wales,

> **Quickies**
> *Did you know ...*
> • that the capitals of five Canadian provinces are, or were, named after royalty — Charlottetown, Prince Edward Island; Fredericton, New Brunswick; Toronto (formerly York), Ontario; Regina, Saskatchewan; and Victoria, British Columbia?

Mnemonic Sequence of English/ British/Commonwealth Monarchs

Willie, Willie, Harry, Stee,
Harry, Dick, John, Harry, three;
One, two, three Neds, Richard two,
Harrys four, five, six ... then who?
Edwards four, five, Dick the bad,
Harrys twain and Ned the Lad;
Mary, Bessie, James the Vain,
Charlie, Charlie, James again ...
William and Mary, Anna Gloria,
Four Georges, William and Victoria;
Edward seven next, and then
George the fifth in 1910;
Ned the eighth soon abdicated
Then George the sixth was coronated;
After which Elizabeth
And that's the end until her death.

and have been granted the honour as formal recognition of the fact. Having achieved the status they can display on their products "By Appointment to ..."

What is "dontopedalogy"?

The term was used by Prince Philip, Duke of Edinburgh, to describe the science of "firmly implanting one's foot in one's mouth."

monarchies
in action

What are the most common misconceptions about monarchy?

1) That Canada has ties with the monarchy. Canada does not just have ties, it *is* a monarchy itself. 2) That Canadians send money to Queen Elizabeth II in England. Her Majesty receives no money whatever from Canadians and never has. Expenses entailed by the monarchy are all connected with public duties and ceremonies such as tours and executive acts. 3) That Her Majesty represents the Crown. It is the other way round. A symbol represents a person, not vice versa. 4) That the king gave up the exercise of all royal powers in Canada by the Letters Patent of 1947 reconstituting the office of governor general. The St. Laurent/Diefenbaker governments got the queen to open Parliament in 1957 as did the Trudeau government in 1977. 5) That the Crown is not only the monarch but "a team of governors." The Crown is defined by the Interpretation Act as being Her Majesty the Queen or His Majesty the King as the case may be. The "team of governors" is a political science description of how the Crown works and has no basis in law.

Countries Elizabeth II Crowned Queen of in 1953

- Australia
- Canada
- Ceylon
- New Zealand
- Pakistan
- South Africa
- United Kingdom

Is the idea that "kings reign but do not rule" a fiction?

This expression is used to convey the fact that while laws are enacted in the name of the king/queen (reigns), the political decisions behind them are made by ministers (rules). In most monarchies, including Commonwealth ones, the distinction is not written down in law. Linguistically the two words mean the same thing, as well, but political convention has given them a distinction that is now readily understood.

Is constitutional monarchy only an emasculated form of real monarchy?

People have the idea that all kings were originally absolute. That is incorrect. Medieval monarchs for the most part possessed no standing army, bureaucracy, or adequate revenue. They had power only over the king's personal domain; that is, the lands he himself owned. Their authority over the whole kingdom was recognized, but because it was not based on brute power, their will could not be everywhere enforced. While there were many cases of monarchs abusing power, the concept of the absolute king was both classical and renaissance, and when constitutional monarchy evolved in the 17th through the 20th centuries it was a fulfillment of earlier kingship, not a repudiation or diminution of it. Constitutional monarchy is an advanced version of medieval kingship. Many of its attributes, such as Parliament, habeas corpus, and trial by jury, were medieval innovations.

Current Realms of Queen Elizabeth II

- Antigua and Barbuda
- Australia
- Bahamas
- Barbados
- Belize
- Canada
- Grenada
- Jamaica
- New Zealand
- Papua New Guinea
- St. Christopher and Nevis
- St. Lucia
- St. Vincent and the Grenadines
- Solomon Islands
- Tuvalu
- United Kingdom of Great Britain and Northern Ireland

How did we come to send people to represent us in Parliament?

Between 1275 and 1307, King Edward I of England established the practice of summoning knights from the counties and men from the towns to his High Court of Parliament. These knights and townsmen were to discuss the affairs of the kingdom with the great nobles, who alone had previously met with the king in parliament. The knights and townsmen represented the "communities" of the kingdom — hence the term "House of Commons." King Edward I's Parliament of 1295, with its lords, knights, and townsmen, is known to history as the "Model Parliament," and after 1307, Parliament organized in this way became the distinctive feature of English politics. Ever since, the representation of communities has been one of our chief constitutional principles. It remained only to expand the actual number of people who chose these members of Parliament over succeeding centuries, until in the 20th century universal suffrage was introduced.

Who make up the Parliament of Canada?

Quickies

Did you know ...

- that Canada is, geographically, the largest monarchy in the world?

The Parliament of Canada consists of the reigning queen or king, the Senate, and the House of Commons. It was created in 1867 by the Constitution Act 1867 (formerly the British North America Act 1867), Section 17.

What are the central gates of Parliament Hill in Ottawa called?

They are called the Queen's Gates and face onto Wellington Street. They are only opened for the arrival of the sovereign or the representative of the sovereign, generally at the opening of Parliament for the entrance of the state landau and escort.

What is royal assent?

A nod. Literally. Much as the media loves to talk about monarchs or their representatives having signed bills into law, the historic legislative act was a nod from the throne. Only afterwards did the sovereign or viceregal representative sign anything. Following the nod by the person sitting on the throne, it was announced that the king, queen, governor general, or lieutenant-governor had consented to the bills. With that, the measures instantly became Acts of Parliament or Legislature. The old Norman French formula of assent was *le roi le veult* or "the king wills it" and refusal of assent *le roi s'avisera*, "the king will think it over." The formula for assent to money bills was different. When King George VI gave royal assent to a Commons supply bill in the Senate in Ottawa on May 19, 1939, the clerk of the Senate declared, "His Majesty the King thanks his loyal subjects, accepts their benevolence, and assents to this bill." Since passage of the Royal Assent Act in 2002 the traditional procedure in Canada is followed at least twice each calendar year, once for a supply bill and once for an ordinary bill. On other occasions a written declaration of royal assent is provided to the Speakers of the Senate and Commons who read it out to their respective houses. In either practice the procedure remains the sovereign's legislative act not an executive one.

How did the sovereign give assent in the Scottish kingdom (prior to 1707)?

Prior to the union with England in 1707, Scotland had its own parliament with its own royal traditions. The monarch gave royal assent by touching the bill with the sceptre, the symbol of royal authority.

Which king gave the royal assent in Parliament in person only once in his life?

King George VI, when he met his Canadian Parliament in 1939. He never performed this act in person in any of his other parliaments or legislatures. Queen Victoria was the last monarch to give royal assent in person in Britain and that was in 1854.

Laws Enacted, Proclaimed, or Otherwise Made by Monarchs	
Code of Hammurabi	Hammurabi
Edict of Milan	Constantine "the Great"
Theodosian Code	Theodosius II
Corpus Juris Civilis	Justinian I
Siete Partidas	Alfonso X
Magna Carta	John
Statutes of Winchester, Mortmain	Edward I
Wiślica-Piotrków Statutes	Casimir III "the Great"
Statute of Praemunire	Richard II
Act of Supremacy, Act of Words	Henry VIII
Act of Supremacy	Elizabeth I
Western Charter for Newfoundland	Charles I
Habeus Corpus Act	Charles II
Act of Succession	William III
Constitutional Act 1791	George III
Code Napoléon	Napoleon I
Emancipation of Slaves	William IV
British North America Act	Victoria
Statute of Emancipation of Serfs	Alexander II
Statute of Westminster	George V
Constitution Act 1982	Elizabeth II

Who is Black Rod?

The Gentleman Usher of the Black Rod, in the United Kingdom, or the Usher of the Black Rod, in Canada, is the chief usher to the sovereign or her representative and is seen most frequently as the monarch's messenger at the opening of Parliament. The name comes from the colour of the rod of office that is carried.

What is the mace?

Originally a weapon for the close protection of the sovereign by his or her personal bodyguard, the mace evolved into a symbol of the sovereign's authority in Parliament and other legislative bodies. In the evolution the handle with the crown on it grew larger as the mace's symbolic role increased and its defensive role diminished.

What does the legal maxim "the king can do no wrong" mean?

Not that he is infallible! Nor that wrong is not sometimes done in the king's name. It means that the king countenances no wrong and wishes all wrongs to be corrected. As Jowitt in his *Dictionary of English Law* states: "if an evil act is done, it, though emanating from the king personally, will be imputed to his ministers, for whose acts the king is in no way responsible."

Quickies
Did you know ...
- that a draft accession declaration accompanied Princess Elizabeth on her October 1951 tour of Canada in case her father, the ailing King George VI in London, should have died during the tour?

Who was the first governor general of Canada?

Not Samuel de Champlain as often stated. A governor general is the personal representative of the monarch. The first person in Canada to be so was Daniel de Rémy de Courcelle who became the king's representative when Louis XIV made Quebec a royal province. Champlain was more like the later governors of the Hudson's Bay Company.

What was the Royal Proclamation of 1763?

Issued by the king, it contained George III's policy for incorporating the new territories in North America and the West Indies obtained by the Treaty of Paris into the governance of the royal dominions. It recognized the aboriginal treaty rights and promised a legislature to Quebec.

Who first suggested a federal union of the North American provinces?

It was suggested by the Duke of Kent in 1814. His letter to Jonathan Sewell, Chief Justice and Speaker of the Legislative Council in Lower Canada, anticipating Confederation by over 50 years, was cited by Lord Durham, in his report, and in the Confederation debates.

What carefully recorded words did Sir John A. Macdonald say to Queen Victoria on the eve of Confederation?

Quickies
Did you know ...
- that Canada is one of only three of the queen's realms outside the United Kingdom (where it is called Her Majesty's Most Honourable Privy Council) to have a Queen's Privy Council? The other two Privy Councils are in Jamaica and Northern Ireland.

Queen Victoria granted Macdonald an audience at Buckingham Palace at noon on March 21, 1867. After kneeling and kissing her hand, Sir John told Her Majesty that the purpose of Confederation was "to declare in the most solemn and emphatic manner our resolve to be under the sovereignty of Your Majesty and your family forever."

Who appointed Canada's first foreign representatives?

King George V appointed the Canadian delegate to the League of Nations in 1920 and the Canadian minister to the United States in 1926.

What is a minister in attendance?

When visiting a Commonwealth country of which the queen is sovereign, members of the royal family are always accompanied by a member of the host government, known as the minister in attendance.

Did Queen Elizabeth II "sign over" Canadian independence on April 17, 1982, in Ottawa during the patriation of the Canadian Constitution ceremony on Parliament Hill, as is sometimes claimed?

No, she did not. Queen Elizabeth II is both Queen of the United Kingdom and Queen of Canada. In 1982, she first gave royal assent in London to the Canada Act, passed by the British Parliament, which transferred the last remaining areas of jurisdictions over Canada held by Britain. Her Majesty then travelled to Ottawa, where, as the Queen of Canada, she signed a proclamation accepting these authorities on behalf of Canada and establishing the Constitution Act, 1982. In effect, she transferred powers from herself as the British queen to herself as the Canadian queen.

Has Queen Elizabeth II ever represented Canada abroad?

Yes, on many occasions. As the embodiment of the Canadian State, Her Majesty always represents Canada, as well as all her other realms, at all times. But Elizabeth II has specifically represented Canada in the United States in 1951 (as a princess), 1957, and 1959, and in France in 1984, 1994, and 2007, for example.

Royal Governors General and Chatelaines of Canada

- John, Marquis of Lorne, Governor General of Canada 1878–1883
- Princess Louise, wife of Marquis of Lorne, Chatelaine 1878–1883
- Prince Arthur, Duke of Connaught, Governor General 1911–1916
- Princess Louise, Duchess of Connaught, Chatelaine 1911–1916
- Earl of Athlone, formerly Prince Alexander of Teck, Governor General 1940–1946
- Princess Alice, Countess of Athlone, Chatelaine 1940–1946

51

When did beginning a monarch's reign from the death of his predecessor start?

In British/Commonwealth practice it began with the accession of Edward I to the throne in 1272. Edward was in Palestine when his father died. His return would take months, so the barons put their hands on the old king's coffin, swore allegiance to Edward, and issued a proclamation stating that he reigned "by hereditary succession and by the will and fidelity of the leaders of the realm." The accession of the king who followed Edward took place the day after his father's death. This innovation superseded the old practice of "electing" a king (from among the royal family) and dating his reign from his coronation.

Members of the Royal Family Who Wanted to or Almost Became Governor General of Canada

- Duke of Kent 1811
- Duke of Albany 1881
- Prince Alexander of Teck 1914
- Duke of York 1930
- Duke of Windsor 1921 and 1944
- Duke of York 1990

Are there countries in the Commonwealth which are monarchies but which do not have Queen Elizabeth II as monarch?

There are five: Brunei, Lesotho, Malaysia, Swaziland, and Tonga. Their current monarchs are Sultan Haji Hassanal Bolkiah Mu'izzaddin Waddaulah, King Letsie III, Sultan Mizan Zainal Abidin, King Mswati III, and King George Tupou V, respectively.

Before being unified under a single ruler, did some nations have more than one king?

Ireland had 90 kingdoms, large and small, with three grades of kings. In Norway there were 29 local kings.

What country had more than one king at a time?

Sparta had two kings and was known as a diarchy. In the Irish Free State in 1936, the proclamation of King George VI by error took effect before the time set for the abdication of Edward VIII to become operative had come. For those few hours Ireland had two kings.

Queens Regnant of Scotland/ England/Britain/Commonwealth
- Margaret (Scotland), 1286–1290
- Mary (Scotland), 1542–1567
- Mary I, 1553–1558
- Elizabeth I, 1558–1603
- Mary II, 1689–1694
- Anne, 1702–1714
- Victoria, 1837–1901
- Elizabeth II, 1952–present

What do the Royal House of Spain, the Grand Ducal House of Luxemburg, former royal, imperial, or ducal houses of France, Brittany, Burgundy, Portugal, Naples, Sicily, Hungary, Parma, Etruria, and Brazil, and the Latin emperors of Constantinople have in common?

Unlike the crowns of other kingdoms that have passed through several families, these dynasties were all different *male* lines of the one royal house called after Hugues Capet, king of France in the year 987.

For what imperial reason was Venice founded?

The famed city on the Adriatic was established by Venetians who wanted to remain subjects of the Byzantine emperor rather than the new revived Roman emperor of the West.

Who made the most famous gibe about the Holy Roman Empire?

The Holy Roman Empire saw itself as the successor to the original Roman Empire. The official name was the Holy Roman Empire of the

German Nation and it mainly embraced the Germanic areas of Europe. The sceptic Voltaire said it was neither holy, nor Roman, nor an empire.

How did the king of Hungary categorize the Habsburgs' amazing ability to collect lands, not by war, but through marriage?

Matthias Corvinus of Hungary originated one of history's cleverest tags. It went: "By others let the wars be waged, thou, happy Austria, get engaged!" Perhaps it was envy on his part for, unlike the Habsburgs, Matthias Corvinus pursued the usual means of war to build up his kingdom, defeating both the Turks and the Bohemians in the process. But his success was short-term whereas the Habsburgs' matrimonial aggrandizement continued, bringing them the great Burgundian inheritance and allowing them to flourish until the end of the Holy Roman Empire and even afterwards.

Which two 20th century monarchs saved their countries at moments of grave crisis and peril?

King Victor Emmanuel III of Italy and King Juan Carlos I of Spain did so. In 1943, Italy, one of the Axis powers of the Second World War, was reeling from defeat on land, sea, and air on every front. Benito Mussolini, the Italian dictator-prime minister, stiffened in his resolve by Adolf Hitler, was unwilling and unable to alter course. Using the royal power, Victor Emmanuel III dismissed Mussolini as prime minister, arrested him, and appointed a government that took Italy out of the alliance with Germany and into the Allied camp. The crucial nature of the king's action is understood when the Italian situation is compared with the German. No monarch existed in Germany to dismiss Hitler, and the German führer prolonged the war to its bitter end, ensuring the deaths of millions more victims and bringing about the devastation of his country. Arguments over whether King Victor Emmanuel III should have entrusted the Fascists with office in Italy in the first place — he thought he was preventing civil war in which Mussolini would have seized the government anyway — will never be resolved, but the decision and courage of the king's action in 1943 cannot be denied. Unfortunately, instead of being acclaimed for saving his country, the king's royal house, which the previous century had unified Italy as one state, was made the scapegoat for the Mussolini years. In 1946, in a plebiscite of highly questionable fairness and legality, in which the anti-democratic Communist Party and United States hostility to monarchy played their role, Italy by a very slim majority rejected the monarchy and became a republic.

The second monarch who saved his country was King Juan Carlos I of Spain. On the death of the Spanish dictator, Francisco Franco, in 1975, the monarchy was restored in Spain in the person of Juan Carlos I. After Spain had undergone a savage civil war and nearly 40 years of dictatorship, the restored monarch peacefully reintroduced democracy to the country's political and civil life. After the transition was made, dissidents in the armed forces staged an attempted *coup d'état* on February 23, 1981, filling the streets with troops and taking the Cortes, the Spanish parliament, hostage. The next day, Juan Carlos I appeared on television and broadcast to the country, telling Spaniards he would not tolerate interruption of the newly ratified democratic constitution. As head of the armed forces, the king warned the rebels of the risk of civil war and said he would not abdicate or leave the country and that the only way they would prevail was by shooting him. Faced with the king's bold action and determined resolve, the rebellion collapsed. The king single-handedly saved Spanish democracy.

Modern Monarchies (other than those of Queen Elizabeth II)

- Andorra
- Bahrain
- Belgium
- Bhutan
- Brunei
- Cambodia
- Denmark
- Japan
- Jordan
- Lesotho
- Liechtenstein
- Luxembourg
- Malaysia (elective monarchy)
- Monaco
- Morocco
- Netherlands
- Norway
- Qatar
- Saudi Arabia
- Swaziland
- Sweden
- Thailand
- Tonga
- United Arab Emirates (elective monarchy)
- Vatican City (elective monarchy)

Of what country besides Britain/Commonwealth is "God Save the King" the royal anthem?

"God Save the Queen" inspired many royal anthems around the world but in the case of Norway it was actually adopted as the tune for the Norwegian royal anthem, "Kongesangen." The originally words were written by Henrik Wergeland and the current version was composed by Gustav Jensen for the coronation of King Haakon VII in 1906.

When Norway became independent, the country approached a Highland chieftain about being its king. Why?

The Norwegians offered their throne to The McLeod, Chief of Clan McLeod. Centuries before, the McLeods had been kings of the Isle of Man and claimed to be a branch of the medieval royal house of Norway. (The McLeod declined.)

Quickies
Did you know ...
- that Queen Victoria's Canadian prime minister, Sir John Thompson, died at her dinner table at Windsor Castle?

Canadian Prime Ministers of Queen Elizabeth II
- Louis St. Laurent (1952–1957)
- John Diefenbaker (1957–1963)
- Lester Pearson (1963–1968)
- Pierre Trudeau (1968–1979; 1980–1984)
- Joseph Clark (1979–1980)
- John Turner (1984)
- Brian Mulroney (1984–1993)
- Kim Campbell (1993)
- Jean Chretien (1993–2004)
- Paul Martin (2004–2006)
- Stephen Harper (2006–present)

What is one of the first things we find out about each new American president?

The media always reports on whether the new president has a royal descent. George Bush the elder, on being elected in 1988, was reported as having more royal ancestors than any other United States president. A royal descent was forged for Abraham Lincoln. Barack Obama is said to be the descendant of African kings.

What was Field Marshal Jan Smuts's advice to Princess Frederica of Greece?

Jan Smuts had been a leader of the Boers in the war against Britain but became a staunch supporter of the monarchy after South Africa became a British dominion. He told Princess Frederica, "If a nation does not want a monarchy, change the nation's mind. If a nation does not need a monarchy, change the nation's needs."

monarchy
and the military

How can one tell the seniority of the regiments in the Household Division?

The seniority is indicated by their tunic buttons. The Grenadier Guards (first) have evenly spaced buttons. The Coldstream Guards (second) have pairs of buttons. The Scots Guards (third) have their buttons in groups of three, the Irish Guards (fourth) in groups of four, and the Welsh Guards (fifth) in groups of five. The system is not used in Canada where the regiments copy their British affiliates instead of using Canadian seniority. Thus, the Governor General's Foot Guards are senior to the Canadian Grenadier Guards but they are affiliated with the Coldstream Guards so they have buttons in pairs, and the Canadian Grenadier Guards wear evenly spaced buttons although they are junior.

The foot guards in London mount a guard in front of Buckingham Palace. Why are there also two mounted troops of the Household Cavalry at the Horse Guards building on Whitehall Road?

While it appears to visitors that the grounds of Buckingham Palace begin at the gates of the palace, all of St. James's Park in front of the palace and Horse Guards Parade up to Admiralty Arch and Trafalgar Square is actually part of the grounds of the palace, though open to the public. The central gateway through the Horse Guards building, not Admiralty Arch, is the official entrance to the grounds, so the mounted troops are guarding the entrance to the grounds of the palace and the foot guards are guarding the palace within the grounds.

> **Quickies**
> *Did you know ...*
> * that the celebrated bearskin headdresses used by the Queen's Guards regiments are made from Canadian bears?

Why is there a changing of the guard in Ottawa?

After Queen Elizabeth II came to the throne in 1952, she adopted the separate style and title "Queen of Canada." Lieutenant General Guy Simonds, Chief of the Canadian General Staff, advised that in keeping with the queen's new style, a regiment of Canadian Guards be created. This took place in 1953. When the queen took up residence at Government House, Ottawa, in the summer of 1959, a mounting and changing of the guard similar to that carried out at Buckingham Palace was arranged. It proved such a popular spectacle that it has been continued ever since during the summer months of the year. To allow as many people as possible to view the ceremony, the changing takes place on Parliament Hill before the guard marches to Rideau Hall to mount guard.

Why is the ceremonial troop of the Royal Horse Artillery known as the King's Troop and not the Queen's Troop?

In 1939, the last battery of the Royal Horse Artillery was mechanized. King George VI wished, however, that after the war a mounted troop

Royal Colonels-in-Chief in Canada

The colonel-in-chief of a regiment is its (usually royal) patron. They do not have an operational role, but are kept informed of all important activities of the regiment, and pay occasional visits to its operational units. Their chief purpose is to maintain a direct link between the regiment and the royal family.

- Queen Elizabeth II (16 units)
- Prince Philip, Duke of Edinburgh (6 units)
- Prince Charles, Prince of Wales (6 units)
- Prince Andrew, Duke of York (3 units)
- Prince Edward, Earl of Wessex (3 units)
- Princess Anne, Princess Royal (7 units)
- Prince Edward, Duke of Kent (1 unit)
- Prince Michael of Kent (1 unit)
- Princess Alexandra, Hon. Lady Ogilvy (2 units)
- Sophie, Countess of Wessex (1 unit)
- Birgitte, Duchess of Gloucester (1 unit)

Household Regiments of the Queen

- The Life Guards (United Kingdom)
- The Blues and Royals (United Kingdom)
- The Governor General's Horse Guards (Canada)
- The Grenadier Guards (United Kingdom)
- The Coldstream Guards (United Kingdom)
- The Scots Guards (United Kingdom)
- The Irish Guards (United Kingdom)
- The Welsh Guards (United Kingdom)
- The Canadian Guards (Canada) (on supplementary order of battle since 1970)
- The Governor General's Foot Guards (Canada)
- The Canadian Grenadier Guards (Canada)
- The King's Troop, Royal Horse Artillery (United Kingdom) (assigned to household duties)
- The Royal Canadian Mounted Police (Canada) (assigned to household duties)

would be reformed in traditional dress. Through the king's interest, the Riding Troop, Royal Horse Artillery, was created and His Majesty inspected it personally in 1947. While signing the guest book, the king crossed out "Riding Troop" and substituted "The King's Troop." When Queen Elizabeth II came to the throne, she decided that the troop would retain that name in honour of her father's special role in creating it.

Who was the last British/Commonwealth king in combat?

King George II led his troops at the Battle of Dettingen in 1743. Subsequently King William IV, King Edward VIII, and King George VI served in combat before they became monarchs. King George II's action is therefore regarded as the last occasion on which a monarch served in combat. But it has been noted by some that since the home front in the Second World War was also the front line, especially during the blitz on London, King George VI could also be said to have led his people in battle.

What was Queen Victoria's view of honouring the troops?

When she wanted to telegraph a message to her troops in South Africa following the uncertain Battle of Colenso, her private secretary said the sovereign only did so when they had won a victory. Replied Queen Victoria: "And since when have I not been proud of my troops whether in success or defeat? Clear the line!"

Members of the Royal Family Holding the Canadian Forces Decoration

- Queen Elizabeth II (from King George VI)
- Prince Philip, Duke of Edinburgh (from Queen Elizabeth II)
- Prince Charles, Prince of Wales (from Queen Elizabeth II)
- Prince Andrew, Duke of York (from Queen Elizabeth II)
- Princess Anne, Princess Royal (from Queen Elizabeth II)
- Prince Edward, Duke of Kent (from Queen Elizabeth II)
- Princess Alexandra, Hon. Lady Ogilvy (from Queen Elizabeth II)
- The Countess Mountbatten of Burma (from Queen Elizabeth II)

What is the difference in appearance between the modern British and Canadian Victoria Crosses?

As part of its policy of "Canadianizing" its honours system, the Victoria Cross was readopted as a Canadian decoration in 1992. It is almost exactly the same in appearance. However, the Canadian version of the Victoria Cross has the original motto "For valour" translated into Latin, as *Pro valore*, to accommodate Canadian bilingualism by using a neutral third language. Some Latin scholars claim, however, that it is a poor translation, that looks right but is incorrect, and that *Pro valore* actually translates as "For value."

In old age, Queen Victoria created a very personal award for heroism. What was it?

Fired by the valour of her troops in the Boer War, Queen Victoria, who decades earlier instituted the Victoria Cross, the world's most famous honour for gallantry, crocheted eight scarves with the royal cipher VRI cross-stitched in one corner. The scarves were for distinguished soldiers of the Canadian, Australian, South African, and New Zealand forces serving in South Africa. The Canadian commander nominated Private Richard Rowland Thompson, an Irishman who came to Canada in 1897 and had risked his life saving fellow soldiers, for a scarf. It was duly awarded. On Victoria Day 1965, Thompson's family presented the precious scarf to the Canadian War Museum where it is on display.

Why is the gun carriage at a royal funeral drawn by men and not horses?

This practice originated at the funeral of Queen Victoria on February 2, 1901. The weather on that winter's day was so cold that one of the horses, ready to draw the gun carriage with the queen's coffin from Windsor station, shied and snapped the traces. No one knew quite what to do until Prince Louis of Battenburg (husband of one of the queen's granddaughters), with great presence of mind, ordered his sailors to drag the gun carriage along the route using the royal train's communication cord. What began as a makeshift arrangement became a venerable tradition of subsequent royal funerals.

What does NCSM stand for?

Canadian warships are designated Her Majesty's Canadian Ship or HMCS. Following the adoption of official bilingualism in Canada, no designation was officially used in French for Canadian ships. After 1984 this was corrected and HMCS was translated into French as *Navire Canadien de Sa Majesté* or NCSM.

Why do Canadian naval officers drink to the queen's health seated?

Naval Reserve Divisions in Canada with Royal Names
- HMCS Brunswicker (Saint John, New Brunswick)
- HMCS Queen (Regina, Saskatchewan)
- HMCS Queen Charlotte (Charlottetown, Prince Edward Island)
- HMCS York (Toronto, Ontario)

King Charles II dined with the officers of the ship on which he was returning to England in 1660 from exile, to assume the throne that he had legally held since 1649. His health was proposed. As the king rose to accept the toast, he struck his head against one of the low deckhead beams. He immediately declared that all future naval toasts to the sovereign should, for safety's sake, be drunk seated.

What daring royal commando operation was contemplated from Canada?

Sir David Kirke, the half-English half-French adventurer, who captured Quebec for his king in 1629, received a grant of land in Newfoundland from the Crown when he had to restore the spoils of war. At Ferryland in the south-eastern part of the Avalon Peninsula, he took over the mansion abandoned by Lord Baltimore a short while before. When the Great Rebellion against Charles I broke out, Kirke wrote to His Majesty offering him a refuge in Ferryland. To better receive the king, he added towers to his mansion. He busily fitted out a fleet of heavily armed ships with which to invade England in conjunction with the king's cousin, Prince Rupert, to rescue Charles I. In the end, Kirke's plans fell through and the king went to his death on the scaffold.

Did King George VI see combat in the First World War?

As the second son of the king, and not expected to succeed to the throne, Prince Albert (as King George VI was then known) was not kept out of harm's way. He was a serving officer in the Royal Navy aboard HMS *Cumberland*, a cruiser. In 1916, the future king's ship fought as part of the Grand Fleet in the famous Battle of Jutland against the German High Seas Fleet.

Quickies

Did you know ...

• that the HMS *Prince of Wales*, the Royal Navy battleship named in honour of the future King Edward VIII, who would abdicate, was considered a "bad luck" ship? It had an accident on launching, was present when HMS *Hood* was blown up by the German battleship *Bismarck*, and then was itself sunk by Japanese aircraft, the first battleship at sea to be destroyed from the air.

Why does the former Royal Yacht *Britannia* (now a museum) have a collapsible mast?

The *Britannia* had a fixed mast when it was constructed in 1952. In 1959, Her Majesty the Queen opened the St. Lawrence Seaway, and the *Britannia* sailed through the Great Lakes with the sovereign on board. The yacht's mast was higher than the hydro wires over the St. Lawrence River section of the seaway. In order to allow the *Britannia* to pass through, the mast was hinged for lowering and raising. It has remained so to this day.

What was the name of the ship that Prince Charles, Prince of Wales, once commanded?

For five years, from the autumn of 1971 until the end of 1976, the Prince of Wales was a serving officer in the Royal Navy. He was posted to HMS *Norfolk*, HMS *Minerva*, and HMS *Hermes* during those

Commonwealth Police Forces with Royal Designations (current)

• The Royal Bahamas Police Force
• The Royal Barbados Police Force
• The Royal Canadian Mounted Police
• The Royal Gibraltar Police
• The Royal Newfoundland Constabulary
• The Royal Virgin Islands Police Force

five years. In 1976, the Prince of Wales's final posting was as commanding officer of the minehunter HMS *Bronington*.

What is a Queen's Colour?

Each infantry regiment in the queen's realms has two colours, or flags. The junior one represents the regiment (the Regimental Colour) and the senior one represents the queen's authority (the Queen's Colour). Except for guards regiments, which reverse the pattern, the former is based on the regimental badge and colours and the Queen's Colour is based on the Royal Union Flag or the National Flag and the regimental badge.

What is the difference between the Yeomen of the Guard and the Yeomen Warders of the Tower?

Yeomen of the Guard are retired non-commissioned officers from the British Army who serve as ceremonial personal guards to the queen on various state functions. Yeomen Warders of the Tower are similarly drawn from retired soldiers but serve only at the Tower of London. Because they were both established by King Henry VIII and still wear Tudor uniforms, they are frequently thought to be the same unit. The confusion was not helped by Gilbert and Sullivan, who wrote their famous operetta about the unit at the tower but erroneously called it *The Yeomen of the Guard*.

Who approved a plot to kidnap the first member of the British royal family in North America?

During the American Revolution, General George Washington, commanding the rebel forces, authorized a 1781 abduction attempt on Prince William (William IV) at New York. The prince was serving with the Royal Navy during the rebellion. The kidnapping failed to come off and Prince William continued his naval career.

> **Quickies**
>
> *Did you know ...*
> * that William IV appointed a son of Benedict Arnold, the American "traitor" but Canadian "Loyalist," as his aide-de-camp?

Is it true that when King George III's army surrendered to the colonial rebels at Yorktown in 1781 they were so disconsolate that their band played "The World Turned Upside Down"?

The band did in fact play the tune used for the song "The World Turned Upside Down," so the story, recounted in American independence mythology, may be true. But the same tune was also the music for another song well known at that time entitled "When the King Enjoys His Own Again," providing the alternative Loyalist belief that the troops surrendered with defiance, not despair.

When was Trooping the Colour on the sovereign's birthday first held?

The Trooping the Colour parade is one of the most recognized ceremonial events held each year in London. To many tourists it is *the* royal event to see. The ceremony is held on the official birthday of the monarch, not the actual birthday. The first trooping on the sovereign's birthday was held in 1785 for the birthday of King George III.

Why was the Duke of Kent's residence in Canada abruptly interrupted in 1794?

Prince Edward, the young major general, was sent at his own request on active service to the West Indies where he commanded a brigade of guards at the taking of Martinique and St. Lucia. On his return to Canada following the successful military expedition, he was promoted to the rank of lieutenant general.

For what occasion was a general amnesty granted to the rebels of 1837?

Various local grievances in Lower Canada led to armed rebellion in 1837. Most of the rebels (such as George Étienne Cartier) remained loyal to the young queen who had just acceded to the throne, however, and insisted they were only resisting local authorities. The following year, to mark the coronation of Queen Victoria on June 28, 1838, a general amnesty was granted to the rebels.

Who thought up the military jackboot?

George T. Denison of Toronto, founder of what became the Governor General's Horse Guards, got the idea from the boots worn by Canadian lumberjacks. His Royal Highness the Duke of Cambridge, Commander-in-Chief of the forces, read about Denison's idea in the latter's book *Modern Cavalry*. The duke had the jackboot adopted for all cavalrymen in Queen Victoria's forces in place of booted overalls.

When did Prince Arthur, Duke of Connaught and governor general of Canada from 1911–1916, first go to Canada?

Prince Arthur, the third son of Queen Victoria, was a professional soldier. In 1869 he was stationed in Canada as an officer with the 1st Battalion, The Rifle Brigade, and fought at the Battle of Eccles Hill against the Fenian invaders of Canada, for which he received the Canadian Fenian Medal. In later years, as governor general, he cited his military service, saying, "I merely mention this as I should not like you to think that I am a relatively Canadian."

Who is the Princess Patricia's Canadian Light Infantry named after?

The regiment was raised in 1914 at the start of the First World War and was the first Canadian regiment to go overseas in that war. It was named after the daughter of the Duke of Connaught, who was governor general of Canada at the time. Princess Patricia was living at Rideau Hall with her parents and was very popular with Canadians. She later gave up her royal title when she married and became known as Lady Patricia Ramsey.

Royal Colonels-in-Chief in the Commonwealth

- Queen Elizabeth II (9 units — 5 Australia, 4 New Zealand)
- Prince Philip, Duke of Edinburgh (2 units — 1 Australia, 1 New Zealand)
- Prince Charles, Prince of Wales (2 units — 1 Australia, 1 Papua, New Guinea)
- Prince Andrew, Duke of York (1 unit — New Zealand)
- Princess Anne, Princess Royal (3 units — 1 Australia, 2 New Zealand)
- Prince Richard, Duke of Gloucester (2 units — 1 Australia, 1 New Zealand)
- Birgitte, Duchess of Gloucester (3 units — 1 Australia, 1 Bermuda, 1 New Zealand)

Which Canadian was knighted by his king on the battlefield?

Sir Arthur Currie, commander of the Canadian Corps, was knighted by George V after the capture of Vimy Ridge in 1917.

Which two Canadian regiments have confusingly similar royal names?

The Royal Canadian Regiment, a regular and reserve force unit based in Petawawa, Ontario, Gagetown, New Brunswick, and London, Ontario, of which Prince Philip, Duke of Edinburgh, is colonel-in-chief and The Royal Regiment of Canada, a reserve unit based in Toronto, of which Prince Charles, Prince of Wales, is colonel-in-chief.

Quickies

Did you know ...

- that Canadian Vivian Tremaine was the nurse who cared for George V during his convalescence from the serious accident he sustained on the Western Front during the First World War?

What organization placed the statue of King George VI at the University of British Columbia?

The local branch of the War Amps of Canada.

Who was Burmese?

She was a black mare, born in 1962, and given to Queen Elizabeth II by the Royal Canadian Mounted Police. The queen rode her for 18 consecutive Trooping the Colour parades on her official birthday in London, from 1969 to 1986. Burmese died in 1990.

Who was the only monarch to be decorated for valour while serving with the British Forces in the field?

King George II of the Hellenes (Greece), a first cousin of the Duke of Edinburgh, was awarded the Distinguished Service Order (D.S.O.) for service in Crete in the Second World War. When the Nazis invaded Greece and seized Athens, King George II and his government went to Crete and organized resistance from there until that island was also overrun.

Canadian Warships Named (Directly or Indirectly) After Royalty

- HMCS *Annapolis* [Second World War destroyer]
- HMCS *Annapolis* (2nd) [post-war destroyer escort]
- HMCS *Charlottetown* [Second World War corvette]
- HMCS *Charlottetown* (2nd) [Second World War frigate]
- HMCS *Charlottetown* (3rd) [current frigate]
- HMCS *Cobourg* [Second World War corvette]
- HMCS *Dauphin* [Second World War corvette]
- HMCS *Fredericton* [Second World War corvette]
- HMCS *Fredericton* (2nd) [current frigate]
- HMCS *Georgian* [Second World War minesweeper]
- HMCS *Guelph* [Second World War corvette]
- HMCS *Kentville* [Second World War minesweeper]
- HMCS *Kingston* [current maritime coastal defence vessel]
- HMCS *Louisburg* [Second World War corvette]
- HMCS *Louisburg* (2nd) [Second World War corvette]
- HMCS *Montreal* [Second World War frigate]
- HMCS *Montreal* (2nd) [current frigate]
- HMCS *Port Arthur* [Second World War corvette]
- HMCS *Port Dauphine* [post-war auxiliary]
- HMCS *Port de la Reine* [post-war auxiliary]
- HMCS *Port St. Louis* [post-war auxiliary]
- HMCS *Prince Rupert* [Second World War frigate]
- HMCS *Regina* [Second World War corvette]
- HMCS *Regina* (2nd) [current frigate]
- HMCS *Royalmount* [Second World War frigate]
- HMCS *Victoria* [current submarine]
- HMCS *Victoriaville* [Second World War frigate]
- HMCS *West York* [Second World War corvette]
- HMCS *Windsor* [current submarine]

pomp
and
pageantry

What does it mean to be "born in the purple"?

This is an expression, now meaning to be well born, given to the language by monarchy. It derives from the Byzantine Empire. The family of the emperor of Byzantium were said to be *porphyrogeniti* — translated "born in the purple." A dynasty of Byzantine emperors was even called the Porphyrogenitus family.

Why are the colours of Canada red and white?

Following the terrible ordeal of the First World War, King George V wished to honour the gallant sacrifice made by his Canadian subjects. He therefore assumed Royal Arms for Canada and, in doing so, assigned red and white as the royal livery colours. Red represented the blood shed by Canadians in the war and white represented the bandages that were also associated with that sacrifice. In later years, when the national flag was adopted for Canada, they were made the colours of the flag.

In addition to being the royal livery colours of Canada, what other royal association is there with the colours red and white?

The red rose was the badge of the Royal House of Lancaster and the white rose the badge of the Royal House of York. The civil war between the two houses is known as the War of the Roses. When the war ended with the victory of the Lancastrian King Henry VII who married Elizabeth of York, the two houses were united as the House of Tudor, and the red and white Tudor Rose became the badge of the royal family and is still in use today throughout the Commonwealth.

Symbols of Monarchs

Double crown, royal uraeus (representation of sacred asp or snake)	Egypt
Lion	Sri Lanka
Umbrella	Assyria, Persia, Tonga
Fleur-de-lys	France
Harp, red hand	Ireland
Ostrich feather fans	Persia
Chrysanthemum	Japan
Peacock	Mogul India, Burma
Wheel	Vedic royalty of India
Triple crown	Papacy
Bundle of arrows	Aragon
Dove	Saxon England
Raven, elephant	Denmark
White hart (deer), broom plant, sunburst, white swan, boar	Plantagenet England
Thistle	Scotland
White eagle	Poland
Pomegranate	Granada
Red dragon	Wales
Double eagle	Holy Roman Empire, Austria, Russia
Golden five-clawed dragon	China
Swan	Bavaria
White rose	Jacobite kings
Bees, violets	Bonapartist France
Maple leaf	Canada
Magen David (first and last letters of name of King David interlaced)	Israel

To which Ontario church did the queen give permission for its clergy and choir to wear red cassocks?

Permission was given to St. Mark's Church in Port Hope. The custom is that royal scarlet can be worn in any church where the sovereign has attended a service. Queen Elizabeth II attended St. Mark's in 1959.

What did kings of Egypt wear that connected their office with its priestly origins?

A mock lion's tail such as is shown on magicians in the prehistoric cave drawings.

How often does Queen Elizabeth II wear her crown?

The queen actually has two crowns. St. Edward's Crown (the coronation crown and the official crown for all Commonwealth realms of the queen) is only worn for a few minutes in her life, at the actual crowning during the coronation ceremony. The Imperial State Crown, based on the design of St. Edward's Crown was also worn by the queen during the coronation and is worn by her at every state opening of Parliament at Westminster. There have been suggestions over the years that comparable state crowns should be created for Canada, Australia, New Zealand, and other realms of the queen for use in those countries, but nothing has yet come of the idea. So the queen wore the tiara passed to her from Queen Alexandra and Queen Mary when she opened the Canadian Parliament in 1957 and 1977.

Crowns in the Tower of London
- St. Edward's Crown, 1661
- Crown of Mary of Modena, 1685
- Prince of Wales' Crown, 1728
- Imperial State Crown, 1837
- Small Crown of Queen Victoria, 1870
- Prince of Wales' Crown, 1901
- Queen Mary's Crown, 1911
- Imperial Crown of India, 1911
- Crown of Queen Elizabeth, The Queen Mother, 1937

What ancient victory song followed coronations of Holy Roman Emperors?

The *Laudes Regiae* or Royal Praises. "Christ conquers! Christ reigns! Christ rules!" Sumerian salutations from the fourth millennium B.C. or earlier turn up in the royal psalms of King David in this hymn that Holy Roman Emperors offered to their Redeemer King after they were anointed and crowned. The *Laudes Regiae* were most recently sung at the installation of Pope Benedict XVI, an elective monarch, in 2005.

What unusual custom was observed at the crowning of kings of Hungary?

The king rode on horseback up a mound of earth created for the occasion from soil brought from every county of the kingdom of Hungary. At the summit he brandished the Sword of St. Maurice, which he had just been invested with, flourishing it at each point of the compass in token of his sovereignty and will to defend the kingdom. The gesture was an appropriate custom for a people who in origin were Asiatic horsemen.

How was the consort of Ethiopian emperors crowned?

Customarily, the empress consort was crowned at the palace in a ceremony entirely separate from that of the emperor. In the modern period, however, the coronation of the empress consort began to take place in church. Emperor Menelik II, for instance, crowned his wife the Empress Taitu on the second day of his five-day coronation festival in the Entoto Marian Church. But not until the reign of Emperor Haile Selassie were the ruler and consort (Empress Menen) crowned together at the Cathedral of St. George in the capital, Addis Ababa.

What is the prototype of the royal throne?

The Throne of Solomon, the true King of Peace in the Bible. Charlemagne's stone-seated throne at Aachen and St. Edward's Chair, with the place for the Stone of Scone, by legend Jacob's pillow, at Westminster Abbey, make a conscious connection with it. At the same time, the throne is the one symbol common to monarchy everywhere. Not all kings and queens had crowns but all possessed a throne.

What did Charles I wear at his coronation?

The king dressed all in white for his crowning, which took place on February 2, 1626. People interpreted Charles I's choice of white as a declaration that he was distancing himself from the moral murkiness of his late father James I's court.

What is the Stone of Scone?

It is the coronation seat of kings of Scotland. The coronation chair (St. Edward's Chair) was built in 1301 to encompass the stone for English coronations after King Edward I captured it in 1296. The stone was kept with the chair at Westminster Abbey between coronations until 1996, when it was moved to Edinburgh Castle.

> **Quickies**
> *Did you know ...*
> * that the *supertunica* (over garment) worn by British/ Commonwealth monarchs at their coronations is modelled on the dress of a consul (and later, emperor) of ancient Rome?

Which of the 1953 coronation regalia was provided by the Commonwealth?

The Armills or Bracelets of Sincerity and Wisdom "for tokens of the Lord's protection embracing you and every side and also for

Coronations from the Tudors

- October 30, 1485 — Henry VII
- June 24, 1509 — Henry VIII
- February 20, 1547 — Edward VI
- October 1, 1553 — Mary I
- January 15, 1559 — Elizabeth I
- July 11, 1603 — James I
- February 2, 1626 — Charles I
- April 23, 1661 — Charles II
- April 23, 1685 — James II
- April 11, 1689 — William III and Mary II
- April 23, 1702 — Anne
- October 20, 1714 — George I
- October 11, 1727 — George II
- September 22, 1761 — George III
- July 19, 1821 — George IV
- September 8, 1831 — William IV
- June 28, 1838 — Victoria
- August 9, 1902 — Edward VII
- June 22, 1911 — George V
- May 12, 1937 — George VI
- June 2, 1953 — Elizabeth II

symbols and pledges of that bond which unites you to your peoples" were presented to Queen Elizabeth II by the Commonwealth countries, replacing the earlier set from the coronation of King Charles II. The bracelets derive from the Scandinavian practice of swearing oaths on a ring and afterwards wearing it. The Commonwealth coronation is the only one in which they have been used from earliest times to the present.

Who carried the Canadian banners in the coronations of 1937 and 1953?

By the Statute of Westminster in 1931 the dominions in the British Empire were recognized as realms of the king equal to the United Kingdom. At the two coronations since then the dominions have had an official role in the ceremony. The banner of the king (1937) and the queen (1953) in right of each dominion was carried in the procession along with the banners for the United Kingdom. These banners were carried by the high commissioners, namely Vincent Massey (1937) and Norman Robertson (1953) for Canada.

Who was the King's Champion?

In coronations from 1377 (King Richard II) to 1820 (King George IV) the King's Champion (an hereditary appointment in the Dymoke family) rode into the dining hall at the coronation banquet on horseback and dressed in armour and challenged any pretender to the throne. "Here is [the King's] Champion" he said "ready in person to combat … and will in this quarrel adventure his life." The banquet has not been held since 1820, but a Dymoke still takes part in the coronation. In 1953, Captain J.L.M. Dymoke carried the Royal Union Banner in the coronation procession in Westminster Abbey.

Have there been English/British/Commonwealth coronations elsewhere than at Westminster Abbey since 1066?

Thirty-nine of the 41 monarchs had coronations held at Westminster Abbey. Two kings were not crowned; King Edward V, murdered in the Tower of London before he was crowned, and King Edward VIII, who abdicated before his coronation. In addition, King Henry III was crowned as a child at Gloucester Cathedral, and again, when older, at Westminster Abbey, King Henry VI was crowned king of France in Paris, and kings James I, Charles I, and Charles II were crowned kings of Scotland (at Stirling, Edinburgh, and Scone respectively), separate from their English coronations.

Was there a Scottish coronation in 1953?

The answer is no, but Queen Elizabeth II was crowned on St. Edward's Chair, underneath which was the Stone of Scone, upon which Scottish kings were traditionally crowned. Following the coronation, the queen travelled to Edinburgh, where she was presented with the Scottish crown jewels (the Honours of Scotland). But she was not invested with them, nor crowned.

What are the "Honours of Scotland"?

This is the name given to the crown jewels of Scotland, which consist of the crown, the sceptre, and the sword of state. They are kept in the

Crown Room at Edinburgh Castle. The crown was remodelled by King James V in 1540 but may date from Robert the Bruce. The sceptre was a gift to King James IV from Pope Alexander VI in 1494, and the sword of state was presented to King James IV by Pope Julius II in 1507.

When was the last Scottish coronation?

The last coronation in Scotland was held in 1651. It was the crowning of King Charles II, who was fighting to obtain the thrones to which by law he had succeeded the previous year after the judicial murder of his father, King Charles I, by Cromwell. The ceremony took place at Scone on January 1. The Marquis of Argyll, a Covenanter and head of Clan Campbell, placed the ancient Scottish crown on the king's head. At the insistence of the ascendant Presbyterians, the coronation was "purged of superstition," that is to say, there was no anointing. Charles II had to wait to receive the holy unction until his restoration, when he was crowned as king of England at Westminster Abbey on St. George's Day, April 23, 1661.

Quickies

Did you know ...

- that King Edward VII's coronation in 1902 was postponed because the monarch developed appendicitis? Appendicitis, at that time, usually caused death, but the elderly, yet courageous monarch successfully underwent one of the earliest operations for the condition.

When has the Gold State Coach been used during Queen Elizabeth II's reign?

Created in Dublin for King George III in 1762, the Gold State Coach has only been used by Queen Elizabeth II on three occasions — the coronation procession in 1953, and the Jubilee processions in 1977 and 2002.

What is the Australian State Coach?

In 1988, to mark Queen Elizabeth II's bicentennial visit to Australia (celebrating the anniversary of the arrival of the First Fleet of settlers there), Her Majesty was presented with the Australian State Coach. It is similar in design to the Irish State Coach built in 1852. The gift was privately arranged and financed by Jim Frecklington of New South Wales, but with the endorsement of the Australian government. Australian materials were used in its construction, and the design features the Royal Arms of Australia and other Australian heraldic images. The coach is kept at the Royal Mews in London, and is used in royal processions along with the other carriages belonging to the queen.

Who are the Crown Jewellers?

The people responsible for the care and maintenance of the Crown Jewels and preparation of regalia for a coronation are known as the Crown Jewellers. Only two companies have held the title — Rundell, Bridge and Rundell (1830–1843) and Garrod and Company (1843–present).

Which of the royal crowns forms part of Charlottetown's coat of arms?

Charlottetown is the capital city of the province of Prince Edward Island and is named after Queen Charlotte, the consort of King George III. Queen Charlotte's state crown is featured in the city's coat of arms.

What is distinctive about the Serbian crown?

The rim of the Serbian crown is decorated with the double-headed silver Serbian eagle with shield of arms. The eagle, suggesting a link with Byzantium, was the emblem of the Royal House of Karageorgevich, founded by George Petrovich, known as Kara George (Black George), the first hereditary prince of modern Serbia, in 1804. The crown is made of brass from cannon captured by Kara George himself when he led the Serbs in rebellion against the occupying Turks. The crown was created for King Peter I, Kara George's descendant, in 1904.

When have kings worn crowns besides coronations and openings of Parliament?

In the Middle Ages, monarchs had ritual crown-wearing days when they appeared in crowns and robes and other attributes of majesty and authority. Edward "the Confessor," for example, kept Easter and Christmas as crown-wearing days. In Slavic kingdoms the Feast of the Assumption of Our Lady was another day for this practice. Royal weddings were also an occasion for it. Usually a high ecclesiastic placed the crown on the sovereign's head on the occasion. Crown-wearing suffered an eclipse in the 12th and 13th centuries.

What was the crown of the Caucasian kingdom of Georgia called?

The Crown of King David III "the Renovator," who reigned from 1089 to 1125. The crown belonged to the Bagratid dynasty, which ruled Georgia as monarchs from 888 until the realm was annexed to the Russian Empire in 1810, and was kept at the Galati Monastery, where it is known to have been at the end of the 19th century. Since then it has been mysteriously lost.

How did the Danish kings come to their coronations?

Already crowned! After the Danish monarchy was declared to be hereditary in the House of Oldenburg in 1660, Danish kings arrived for anointing in the Chapel of Fredericksborg Castle already wearing their crown and other regalia. The reason for this was that because supreme spiritual authority was vested in the post-Reformation kings, it was considered unfitting for them to receive their crowns at the hands of another person.

What was the Romanian crown made of?

Its name gives the answer. The crown was called the *Couronne d'Acier* and was fashioned from the steel of a Turkish gun captured in the War of Independence in which Romania secured its freedom from the Ottoman Empire. The Couronne d'Acier was used for the coronation of the first king of modern Romania, Charles I, in 1881, and by his successor, King Ferdinand I, whose coronation took place at Alba Julia in 1922 to mark the creation of greater Romania through the incorporation of the former Hungarian province of Transylvania.

What Canadian precious stone was kept with the Crown Jewels?

A large piece of amethyst from Cape Blomidon, Acadia (Nova Scotia), was kept by Henri IV with the French Crown Jewels.

What is the "Last Spike" brooch?

It was a brooch given to the Crown in 1987 by the Reford family, descendants of Lord Mount Stephen, first president of the Canadian Pacific Railway. The spike that was to have been the last spike in the CPR at Craigellachie, British Columbia, was bent when struck and was replaced. Lord Mount Stephen was given the damaged spike as a souvenir and he turned it into three jewelled brooches for ladies in his family. One of these was passed down to the Reford family, which donated it to be part of the "regalia" of Canada.

Famous Crowns

St. Stephen's Crown	Hungary
Iron Crown of Lombardy	Italy
Theodelinda's Crown	Italy
Reichskrone	Holy Roman Empire/Germany
Hauskrone of Rudolf II	Holy Roman Empire/Austria
Pahlavi Crown	Iran/Persia
Kamelaukion	Byzantium
Eric IV's Crown	Sweden
Silver Crown of Tewadros	Ethiopia
Crown of László II	Hungary
Imperial Nuptial Crown	Russia
Great Monomakh Cap	Russia
Crown of Astrakhan	Russia
Crown of Louis XV	France
Imperial Crown of Catherine II	Russia
Crown of Augustus III	Poland
St. Edward's Crown	England/Britain/Commonwealth
Imperial State Crown	Britain/Commonwealth
State Diadem of Mary of Modena	England/Britain/Commonwealth
State Diadem of George IV	Britain/Commonwealth
Queen Victoria's Small Diamond Crown	Britain/Commonwealth
Queen Mary's Crown	Britain/Commonwealth
Imperial Crown of India	Britain/Commonwealth
Funeral Crown of Louis XVIII	France
Kalakaua's Crown	Hawaii
Tongan Crown	Tonga
Crown of Otto I	Greece
Triregnum or Tricorona of Leo XIII	Papacy
Crown of Peter I	Yugoslavia

Crown of William II	Prussia
Couronne d'Acier	Romania
Queen Marie's Crown	Romania
Crown of Reccesvinthus	Spain

Why was a new crown made for the investiture of the Prince of Wales in 1969?

The coronet used for the investiture in 1911 was considered too theatrical, the 1728 Prince of Wales' Crown too fragile, and the 1901 Prince of Wales' Crown had been kept by the Duke of Windsor when he abdicated and was not returned until after his death in 1972.

Is there an actual Canadian throne?

The official throne of the queen in the United Kingdom is the chair in the House of Lords and, similarly, the official Canadian throne of the queen is the chair in the Senate. It dates from the 19th century and survived the great fire of 1916 that destroyed the original parliament buildings centre block in which the Senate Chamber is housed. The Royal Arms of the time are displayed on the back of the throne.

What two historic royal dresses is the Canadian Museum of Civilization custodian of?

The dress worn by Queen Elizabeth when she and King George VI met Parliament in 1939, and the "maple leaf" dress Queen Elizabeth II wore on her 1959 tour are kept at the museum

Where is the largest stone-carved Royal Arms in the Commonwealth?

Rideau Hall grew in a haphazardly fashion as the Ottawa residence of the sovereign and the sovereign's representative. New wings were added at different times. The front façade of Rideau Hall, constructed in 1913 at the same time as the modern front façade of Buckingham Palace, which it resembles, boasts, over the ceremonial entrance, the largest depiction of the Royal Arms in any of the countries of the Commonwealth.

What famous Canadian hotel displays the arms of King George V, Queen Mary, and other members of his family?

The Fairmount Royal York in Toronto opened in 1929 and the anteroom of the Imperial Room featured coats of arms of the royal family. In later years the arms were painted over but recent restoration has returned them to their original condition.

The Queen's Beasts (1953 Coronation)

- Crowned Lion of England (Queen Elizabeth II)
- Griffon of King Edward III (House of Windsor)
- Silver Falcon of the Plantagenets (House of York)
- Black Bull of Clarence (House of York)
- White Horse of Mortimer (House of York)
- Yale of Beaufort (House of Lancaster)
- Greyhound of Richmond (House of Lancaster)
- Red Dragon of Wales (House of Tudor)
- Unicorn of Scotland (House of Stuart)
- White Horse of Hanover (House of Hanover or Brunswick)

What is a herald?

He or she is an officer of the queen who belongs to the College of Arms (England), the Court of Lord Lyon (Scotland), or the Canadian Heraldic Authority, and is responsible for exercising the queen's heraldic authority in granting coats of arms to persons and corporate bodies and supervising heraldic matters in his or her jurisdiction.

Who established the College of Arms and the Canadian Heraldic Authority?

The College of Arms and the Canadian Heraldic Authority are two of the bodies that exercise the queen's heraldic authority in granting coats of arms. King Richard III granted the College of Arms a charter in 1484 and Queen Elizabeth II authorized the creation of the Canadian Authority in 1988.

What royal myth inspired the creation of the Order of the Garter?

King Edward III established the Most Noble Order of the Garter, the premier order of chivalry in the Commonwealth, in 1348. The order was inspired by the saga of King Arthur and the Knights of the Round Table. The saint chosen as its patron was St. George, whose role as protector of soldiers was connected with the Crusades. *Honi soit qui mal y pense* or "Shame on him who thinks this evil" is the Order's motto.

What are Royal Family Orders?

Dating from the reign of King George IV, the Orders are badges with miniature portraits granted by the sovereign to female members of the royal family. Marriage into the royal family does not automatically bestow the Order. Although Diana, Princess of Wales, received the Order, Sarah, Duchess of York, did not, nor has Princess Michael of Kent.

Quickies

Did you know ...

- that the motto of the Queen's Order of Canada, *Desiderantes Meliorem Patriam* ("They desire a better country"), is taken from Hebrews 11:16 in the Bible — "But they desire a better country, that is, an heavenly one: wherefore God is not ashamed to be called their God; for he hath prepared for them a city"?

The Queen's Canadian Beasts

While there is no official grouping of Queen's Beasts for Canada separate from those used at the coronation in 1953, the following are used as supporters or crests in the Queen's Royal Arms in right of Canada, the Provinces, and the Territories, and may be considered as part of the Dominion's heraldic menagerie.

- Antelope (Alberta)
- Beaver (Alberta, Manitoba, Saskatchewan)
- Bear (Ontario)
- Bighorn Ram (British Columbia)
- Blue Jay (Prince Edward Island)
- Caribou (Nunavut)
- Deer (Ontario, New Brunswick, Saskatchewan)
- Elk (Newfoundland and Labrador)
- Fox (Prince Edward Island)
- Horse (Manitoba)
- Lion (Alberta, British Columbia, Canada, Saskatchewan)
- Malamute (Yukon)
- Moose (Ontario)
- Narwhal (Northwest, Nunavut)
- Salmon (New Brunswick)
- Unicorn (Canada, Manitoba, Nova Scotia)
- Wapiti Stag (British Columbia)

Why was the maple leaf chosen as the national badge of Canada?

The maple leaf became Canada's national badge in direct consequence of the tour of British North America by the Prince of Wales (later King Edward VII) in 1860. It was in that year, during the public planning for the royal tour, that native-born Canadians voiced their desire for a badge to wear when welcoming the prince, to match the English rose, Scottish thistle, Welsh leek, Irish shamrock, or French lily. By general consensus, the maple leaf was adopted. Knowing of this, the prince brought tableware with him decorated with maple leaves to use on his tour and as gifts. Later he gave the maple leaf official recognition as a royal badge by incorporating it into the design for his coronation invitation cards. Subsequently the maple leaf was introduced into the Royal Arms of Canada and from there into the National Flag.

Why is a crowned lion holding a maple leaf in its paw used as the symbol of the governor general of Canada?

The crowned lion holding a maple leaf in its paw is the crest of the Queen's Royal Arms of Canada. It is a Canadian variation of the lion crest on the Queen's Royal Arms for the United Kingdom. The crests of coats of arms are frequently used to identify the staff or property of the person who possesses the coat of arms; thus the governor general uses the queen's Canadian crest as a badge to indicate that she is one of Her Majesty's staff as her representative in Canada. The same badge of the Canadian royal lion is used as the cap badge for all colonels in the Canadian Armed Forces in a similar fashion.

What are the Prince of Wales' Feathers?

The feathers are actually the heir to the throne's feathers, not the Prince of Wales', as they are the badge of the heir, whether or not he has been created Prince of Wales. Originally it is thought the badge of the king of Bohemia, the three ostrich feathers encircled by a coronet and the motto *Ich Dien* was, according to tradition, adopted by Edward, Prince of Wales (the Black Prince) after he defeated the king in battle.

What is inscribed on the baton of the Speaker of the Canadian House of Commons?

The baton is a symbol of office carried on ceremonial occasions by the Speaker. It is inscribed with the words *Pro regina et patria* ("For queen and country").

How was the State Landau of Canada acquired?

Earl Grey, Governor General of Canada, 1904–1911, bought the landau from the governor general of Australia and brought it with him to Canada. When his time as governor general ended, he left the landau in Ottawa to be the permanent official carriage. By the end of the Second World War it was no longer in use. It was brought back into service by Vincent Massey in the 1950s, when he became governor general, and it remains in use today.

What spoils of battle did Queen Victoria send to Canada to mark the victorious end of the Crimean War?

Queen Victoria sent cannon taken at Sebastopol, similar to the one from which the Victoria Crosses are made. They are found in Toronto, Hamilton, and Montreal. The two in Toronto are located in front of the Provincial Parliament Building at Queen's Park.

Which Canadian schools were given banners worked by royal ladies?

The University of Toronto received a banner showing the Black Prince receiving the banner of the king of Bohemia from King Edward III done by the Princess of Wales (Queen Mary). The second went to Villa Maria Convent School, Montreal, which was given a banner also done by the princess, who had visited the school. And the third was Royal Victoria College, McGill University, endowed with The Queen's Banner, probably worked by Queen Alexandra.

Quickies

Did you know ...

- that King George VI's coronation took place on the same day scheduled for the coronation of his brother King Edward VIII, who abdicated six months before?

Where in Manitoba is there a cairn that commemorates the 1937 coronation of King George VI and Queen Elizabeth?

The cairn is located at Gimli, a community of Icelandic immigrants, north of Winnipeg. At the top of the cairn is a silver coloured oval medallion of George VI and Elizabeth wearing their crowns.

What honour did kings and queens bestow on aboriginal leaders?

Leaders were presented with large silver chiefs' medals bearing the sovereign's image. When Chief Sitting Bull came north to Canada seeking sanctuary from Queen Victoria following the battle at the Little Big Horn against the American cavalry, he was wearing one of the medals, which he showed to the North West Mounted Police. It depicted the image of King George III, grandfather of Queen Victoria. Sitting Bull explained that it had been given to his ancestor by the king for fighting as an ally of His Majesty against the American rebels in the American Revolution a century before, and had been passed down to him.

What is "court mounting" of orders, decorations, and medals?

Court mounting was introduced at the command of King George V, who thought dangling medals looked sloppy, and it is the practice in Commonwealth countries. The insignia (ribbon and medal) are glued to a stiff backing, which is then pinned to the wearer's jacket.

In which religious tradition is the wedding ceremony a coronation?

Each Orthodox or Byzantine Christian bride and groom is crowned at their wedding. This royal act reflects the belief of the world's second largest Christian community that every husband and wife are a king and queen — of creation because they are fellow workers with God, and of love because they are called in their marriage to do their part to make the world a more loving place.

Royal Jubilees Celebrated

- 1809 — King George III (Golden)
- 1887 — Queen Victoria (Golden)
- 1897 — Queen Victoria (Diamond)
- 1935 — King George V (Silver)
- 1977 — Queen Elizabeth II (Silver)
- 2002 — Queen Elizabeth II (Golden)

91

Which British/Commonwealth princes were married in a Russian Orthodox wedding as well as an Anglican ceremony?

This distinction belongs to Alfred, Duke of Edinburgh, second son of Queen Victoria, who married the Russian Grand Duchess, Marie, and George V's third son Edward, Duke of Kent, who married Princess Marina of Greece.

royal
residences

From which palace in England do heralds proclaim the accession of a new sovereign?

The proclamation of the new sovereign is read from the balcony of St. James's Palace by the Garter King of Arms. St. James's, though little remains of the buildings acquired and rebuilt by Henry VIII thanks to a devastating fire in 1810, is the official residence of the monarch in London. The accession proclamation is also read from other locations in London, in Edinburgh, and in the capitals of the sovereign's other realms.

> **Quickies**
> *Did you know ...*
> • that the royal residences at Thebes of the Egyptian Pharaohs were the earliest know palaces?

What is the connection between the Seven Hills of Rome and monarchy?

The seven hills on the east side of the Tiber River form the heart of Rome within the ancient walls. It was here that Romulus is said to have founded the city. The seven, in a clockwise spiral, are the Capitoline Hill, Quirinal Hill, Viminal Hill, Esquiline Hill, Caelian Hill, Aventine Hill, and Palatine Hill. Capitoline Hill, which became the site of the Senate, is the source for the American name for their legislative building — the Capitol. Palatine Hill was the site of the executive and is the root of the word *palace* for a royal residence. A royal mnemonic can also be used to remember the sequence of the hills — Can Queen Victoria Eat Cold Apple Pie.

> **Quickies**
> *Did you know ...*
> • that although the queen does not live there, St. James's Palace, not Buckingham Palace, is the official home of the sovereign in London, and that is why foreign ambassadors are accredited to the Court of St. James's?

What is Government House?

Government House is the official term used in the Commonwealth to designate the residence of the sovereign's representative. The designation is used whether the governor is a direct representative of the sovereign (governors general or state governors in Australia) or an indirect representative (Canadian provincial lieutenant-governors who represent the queen but are appointed by the governor general). Some government houses are also known by their particular names, such as Rideau Hall in Ottawa.

Is there a government house in every province in Canada?

Originally there was a government house in every province, but no longer. In British Columbia, Manitoba, Newfoundland and Labrador, Nova Scotia, and Prince Edward Island there are government houses that are also residences for the viceroys. Alberta, New Brunswick, and Saskatchewan maintain their historic government houses for official purposes, in which the lieutenant-governors have offices but no living accommodation. Ontario and Quebec, the two largest provinces, do not maintain government houses. The lieutenant-governor of Ontario has a non-residential suite at Queen's Park, the provincial legislature.

Some Regal Castles of Europe

- Akershus Castle (Oslo, Norway)
- Alhambra (Granada, Spain)
- Bastille (Paris, France)
- Bran Castle [Dracula's Castle] (Bran, Romania)
- Caernarvon Castle (Caernarvon, Wales)
- Dublin Castle (Dublin, Ireland)
- Edinburgh Castle (Edinburgh, Scotland)
- The Royal Castle (Cracow, Poland)
- Harlech Castle (Harlech, Wales)
- Hohenzollern Castle (Stuttgart, Germany)
- Kalmar Castle (Kalmar, Sweden)
- Neuschwanstein Castle (Hohenschwangau, Germany)
- Peter and Paul Fortress (St. Petersburg, Russia)
- Tower of London (London, England)
- Windsor Castle (Windsor, England)

Where was the first Prince of Wales proclaimed?

King Edward I presented his infant son, the future King Edward II, to the people of Wales from the ramparts of Caernarvon Castle. This act was an attempt by the king, who had just conquered the principality, to reconcile the people to his authority by giving his heir the title of

Prince of Wales. Although the first prince was actually invested subsequently in Lincoln, the modern Investitures at Caernarvon Castle of Prince Edward (1911) and Prince Charles (1969) as Prince of Wales were a revival of the beginnings of the title.

Which famous queen consort lived at Glamis Castle, which figures prominently in William Shakespeare's play *Macbeth*?

Queen Elizabeth, the consort of King George VI and more familiarly known as Queen Elizabeth, the Queen Mother, lived at Glamis, the ancestral castle of her family, the Strathmores.

Some Former Royal Residences

- Brighton Pavilion (King George IV, when Prince of Wales)
- Osborne House (Queen Victoria)
- Marlborough House (King Edward VII, when Prince of Wales)
- Fort Belvedere (King Edward VIII, when Prince of Wales and King)
- 145 Piccadilly (King George VI, when Duke of York)
- Royal Yacht *Britannia* (Queen Elizabeth II)

What is the connection between Hampton Court Palace and the Bible?

Hampton Court Palace was the site of the conference established by King James I, which led to the authorized English translation known as the King James Bible.

What is distinctive about the architecture of Hampton Court Palace?

One side of the palace is in Tudor architecture and the other facing the gardens, built by King William III, is in classical style. The two sides almost seem to be two separate palaces joined together.

What was once the largest palace in Europe?

Whitehall Palace, created by King Henry VIII in 1530 and demolished in 1698, covered 23 acres. By comparison, Buckingham Palace covers nine acres, Versailles seven acres, and the Escorial three acres. As the sovereign's palace it was also the home of all government departments in its time. As a result the term "Whitehall" is still used to colloquially refer to the British government in general.

How did the Royal Mews get its name?

The home of the royal stables and royal automobiles was originally the location of the mewing (changing of plumage) grounds for the royal falcons. The site was then rebuilt as horse stables, and ultimately automobiles as well as carriages have been stored there.

Some Famous Palaces of Europe

- Amalienborg Palace (Copenhagen, Denmark)
- Apostolic Palace (Vatican City)
- Buckingham Palace (London, England)
- Charlottenburg Palace (Berlin, Germany)
- Doge's Palace (Venice, Italy)
- Grand Kremlin Palace (Moscow, Russia)
- The Residenz (Munich, Germany)
- Holyroodhouse Palace (Edinburgh, Scotland)
- Huis ten Bosch Palace (Den Haag, Netherlands)
- Louvre Palace (Paris, France)
- Royal Palace of Madrid (Madrid, Spain)
- Sanssouci Palace (Potsdam, Germany)
- Schonbrunn Palace (Vienna, Austria)
- Versailles Palace (Versailles, France)
- Winter Palace (St. Petersburg, Russia)

Which is the last royal castle to be built in Britain?

The foundation stone for Balmoral Castle, a private home of the queen, was laid in 1853 and the building was completed in 1856. Balmoral was the creation of Prince Albert, the prince consort who acquired the property from the Earl of Aberdeen. An original castle stood on the property and dated from the 15th century but it was demolished when the new one was finished.

British Royal Family Residences

- Prince of Wales:
  Official: Clarence House and St. James's Palace (London residence)
  Private: Highgrove [Gloucestershire]; Birkhall [Aberdeenshire];
    Llwynywermod [Wales]; Tamarisk [Isles of Scilly]
- Duke of York:
  Official: Buckingham Palace (London residence); The Royal Lodge
    [Windsor, Berkshire] (country residence)
- Earl of Wessex:
  Official: Buckingham Palace (London residence); Bagshot Park [Surrey]
    (country residence)
- Princess Royal:
  Official: St. James's Palace (London residence)
  Private: Gatcombe Park [Gloucestershire]

Was Buckingham Palace bombed in the Second World War?

Yes, it was bombed twice in 1940. On the second occasion the king and queen were in the palace but were unhurt even though the bomb fell just 30 yards away from them. The palace chapel was destroyed by the bombing, and it was replaced after the war by the current Queen's Gallery and a smaller private chapel. The queen remarked after the attack that she was glad to have been bombed, "Now I can look the East End in the face," referring to the working-class part of London that had borne the brunt of the Luftwaffe's assault.

Which was Queen Elizabeth the Queen Mother's favourite home?

The Castle of Mey in Scotland, which she purchased in 1953, after the death of the king, remained her favourite home for the rest of her life. It is in Caithness, on the north coast of Scotland. It was in a state of disrepair when acquired and the Queen Mother restored it as a holiday home, staying there every August and October, including 2001, just before her death in early 2002. In 1996 she transferred the property to the Queen Elizabeth Castle of Mey Trust, which opened the castle and grounds to the public following the Queen Mother's death.

Quickies

Did you know ...

- that Buckingham House was bought by King George III as a private country residence for his wife, Queen Charlotte, and known as "The Queen's House" before it was rebuilt as Buckingham Palace?

What monument did Queen Mary unveil in 1913 by pressing a button at Buckingham Palace?

New technology allowed the queen to unveil the tower to mark the centenary of the Battle of Stoney Creek (1813), one of the decisive conflicts of the War of 1812, from the other side of the Atlantic Ocean.

What room in the Parliament Buildings features Canada's French kings?

In 1993, the original smoking room of the Senate, which had been converted into a meeting and reception room, was officially renamed *Le Salon de la Francophonie* — "The Francophonie Room." It was subsequently decorated with portraits of five Canadian monarchs from the French regime — Kings Francois I, Henri IV, Louis XIII, Louis XIV, and Louis XV and a décor featuring fleurs-de-lys. The paintings were donated by Senator Serge Joyal.

Where is the headquarters of the Commonwealth Secretariat?

Queen Elizabeth II gave the secretariat the use of Marlborough House in London. Marlborough House had been the London home of King Edward VII when he was the Prince of Wales and his friends were known as the "Marlborough House Set."

Where are the Canada Gates?

The impressive and ornate Canada Gates are just outside Buckingham Palace, north of the Victoria Memorial, and lead to Green Park. They were erected in 1906 and partly paid for by the people of Canada as part of the refurbishment of the palace carried out under the supervision of King Edward VII. The gates have the coats of arms of the (then) six armigerous provinces and their shields conjoined as the de facto armorial bearings of the Dominion. Newfoundland in 1906 was itself a dominion, so next to the Canada Gates is the Newfoundland Gate. The symbolism of these portals to the palace is that it is the working residence of the queen of Canada as much as of the sovereign of the United Kingdom.

Quickies

Did you know ...

- that Chorley Park, which served as Government House in Toronto, Ontario, from 1912 to 1937, and was demolished in 1961, was described as the grandest governor's residence north of Mexico?

Which royal residence has a room panelled in Canadian maple?

The Duke of Edinburgh's former sitting room in Clarence House is lined with white maple given by Canada to Princess Elizabeth and the duke for their wedding in 1947. The duke's desk was also made in Canada of the same material.

What hideaway did King George VI and Queen Elizabeth rest in on the 1939 tour?

Outlook Cabin, a lodge in Jasper Park, Alberta, was used by the royal couple for a one day "holiday" at the midway point of their historic tour of Canada in 1939. The king and queen so liked the spot that the king remarked, "Oh, if only we could stay here."

Quickies

Did you know ...

- that Kent House on St. Louis Street, where the Duke of Kent (father of Queen Victoria) lived within the walls of Quebec City, still stands and is currently used as the consulate of France?

In his days in Canada, the Duke of Kent (father of Queen Victoria) had two country houses. Where were they?

One was a house at Montmorency Falls, Quebec, which His Royal Highness rented from General Sir Frederick Haldimand. The other, called Prince's Lodge, was on the Windsor Road (now called Bedford Highway) outside Halifax. Prince's Lodge has been demolished but the Duke's Rotunda or Bandstand on the site survives.

What and where is Hatley Castle?

Hatley Castle is located in Colwood, a suburb of Victoria, British Columbia. It was built as a private residence in 1906 by James Dunsmuir, Lieutenant-Governor of British Columbia, and is now the site of Royal Roads University. Formerly it was Royal Roads Military College and the Naval College of the Royal Canadian Navy. The Canadian government, however, did not originally purchase it for the Armed Forces. It was acquired as a home for King George VI, Queen Elizabeth, Princess Elizabeth, and

Quickies

Did you know ...

- that King William IV, who died before it was ready for occupancy, so disliked the prospect of living in Buckingham Palace that he tried to turn it over to the British Museum as an art gallery?

101

Princess Margaret if they were evacuated from Britain during the Second World War. The Canadian government urged the monarchs and the two princesses to come and live in Canada to escape the perils of enemy bombardment in those bleak days. The king refused to leave, however, and the castle was put to its subsequent uses.

Which monarchs of Canada have stayed at Rideau Hall?

Four monarchs have stayed at the sovereign's Ottawa home since it was acquired by the Crown. A fifth visited the grounds. In 1860, when it was still a private residence, King Edward VII (then Prince of Wales) drove through the grounds. King George V stayed at the Hall in 1882 (as Duke of York) and in 1901 and 1908 as Prince of Wales and Duke of York. King Edward VIII was in residence as Prince of Wales in 1919, 1923,

Names of the Queen's Official Castles, Palaces, and Government Houses

- Windsor Castle: Windsor, England
- St. James's Palace: London, England
- Buckingham Palace: London, England
- Holyroodhouse Palace: Edinburgh, Scotland
- Rideau Hall: Ottawa, Canada
- La Citadelle: Quebec City, Canada
- Yarralumla: Canberra, Australia
- Admiralty House: Sydney, Australia
- Government House: Wellington, New Zealand
- The Parsonage: Saint John's, Antigua, and Barbuda
- Government House: Nassau, Bahamas
- Government House: Bridgetown, Barbados
- Government House: Belmopan, Belize
- Government House: St. George's, Grenada
- Government House: Kingston, Jamaica
- Government House: Port Moresby, Papua, New Guinea
- Springfield House: Basseterre, St. Christopher and Nevis
- Government House: Castries, St. Lucia
- Government House: Kingstown, St. Vincent and the Grenadines
- Government House: Honiara, Solomon Islands
- Government House: Funafuti, Tuvalu

1924, and 1927. King George VI was present as Prince Albert in 1913 and returned as king in 1939, the first monarch to be in residence as sovereign. Gustave Lanctot, the official historian of the 1939 tour, wrote, "When Their Majesties walked into their Canadian residence, the Statute of Westminster had assumed full reality, the King of Canada had come home." Queen Elizabeth II arrived in 1951 as Princess Elizabeth and has returned to her Canadian home numerous times since her first residence as sovereign in 1957.

How did one provincial lieutenant-governor humorously explain his name and role to schoolchildren?

The lieutenant-governor, using a play on the Canadian pronunciation of lieutenant (*lef* - tenant), said that the queen owns the government house he lived in. But when she was not in residence he was "left tenant" and looked after the building for her as her governor.

crown
and culture

How has kingship permeated culture?

Consider some names, terms, and expressions: Fit for a king!; king of beasts, King of the Castle; kingpin; king's peace; king's ransom; king crab; King's court; a royal welcome; "a cat may look at a king"; king of the jungle; king's evil; kingfisher; we treat you royally; *bateau du roi* (Canadian flat-bottomed river boat); King of Terrors; King of Heaven; king post; King Charles spaniel; king's spear; King's Counsel; King's highway; King's Bench; king's bargain; King's shilling; king bolt; royal flush; kingcraft; king of spades; royal icing; kingcup; royal fern; royal mast; kingbird; kingfish; royal tennis; royal stag; royal plural; royal

Famous Monarchical Patrons	
Saul	David
Philip II	Aristotle
Charlemagne	Alcuin
Leo X	Raphael
Julius II	Michelangelo
François I	Leonardo da Vinci
Charles X	Titian

road to; royal blue; royal jelly; royal burgh; Queen of Heaven; queen bee; Queen's Counsel; queen of hearts; beauty queen; Dairy Queen; queen of the night; queen post; queen mother; Queen's metal; Queen's pigeon; Queen's Ware; play queen; Queen's delight; Queen of the May; and "queening it."

What is one of monarchy's great bequests to civilization?

The concept of good manners is largely derived from the sovereign's court, which fathered the ideal of the gentleman. The Renaissance Court of Federigo Montefeltro, Sovereign Duke of Urbino, for example, has been called the "mirror school of courtesies." Baladassare Cortegiano's book *The Courtier* was based on life at the Urbino Court and became a pattern book of manners. Since every courtier was outranked by the sovereign, there was a basic equality in the rules of behaviour and deportment that derived from the court, despite its differentiation by office and function. At Versailles, Louis XIV lifted his hat when he met a serving maid in the corridors and slightly raised himself when any lady approached his dinner table. Marie Antoinette apologized when she accidentally trod on the executioner's foot on the scaffold. Queen Victoria was noted for her simple but exquisite manners when visiting the cottages of the poor. George VI was noticed to make his consort Queen Elizabeth precede him during the 1939 Canadian royal tour.

Who are the four kings in a deck of cards?

The four kings of the cardboard court are four legendary and representative monarchs of the world. The king of hearts is the emperor Charlemagne. He is the most majestic, with an abundant show of ermine because Charlemagne was so highly regarded for having revived the Roman Empire in the West. Hearts is always the chief suit and the king of hearts is the king of the pack. The king of spades is King David of the Bible. Spades derives from the Italian word *spada* meaning sword, and David was made the king of spades since he was the man of the sword. The king of diamonds is Julius Caesar (believed in the Middle Ages to have been the first emperor of Rome). The battle-axe held by the king of diamonds evolved from the *fasces* (a bundle of elm or birch rods with a projecting axe blade) of ancient Rome. And the king of clubs is Alexander the Great (King of Macedonia and conqueror of the world). The orb of the king of clubs symbolizes Alexander the Great's conquest of the globe.

Some Operas Involving Monarchy
- *A Life for the Tsar* (Mikhail Glinka)
- *Macbeth* (Giuseppe Verdi)
- *Il Rè pastore* (Mozart)
- *Oedipus Rex* (Igor Stravinsky)
- *Don Carlos* (Giuseppe Verdi)
- *Boris Goudunov* (Modest Mussorgsky)
- *Tristan and Isolde* (Richard Wagner)
- *Prince Igor* (Alexander Borodin)
- *The Tsar's Bride* (Nicholas Rimsky-Korsakov)
- *Aida* (Giuseppe Verdi)
- *Queen of Sheba* (Karl Goldmark)
- *Deirdre of the Sorrows* (Healey Willan)
- *Charles V* (Ernst Křenek)
- *Coronation of Poppaea* (Monteverdi)
- *Prince Charles and Flora* (Healey Willan)

Why is horseracing known as the sport of kings?

Monarchs have always been keenly interested in horseracing — no doubt because of the importance of the horse in war and communications. As early as 1500 B.C. a treatise on the breeding and training of horses was written for a Hittite king. Modern organized racing, however, originated with our own kings and queens. Henry VIII had studs at Hampton Court, Malmesbury, Tutbury, and Ribon. James I was a great patron of the turf in Scotland. When he succeeded to the English throne, he took his passion along with him, and his son Charles I had 139 horses with 32 brood mares at Tutbury in 1649, the year he was murdered. Charles II is known as the "Father of the British turf" and often rode and won both match and plate races at Newmarket. Queen Anne's patronage gave Ascot the high distinction it still retains. Queen Victoria gave her name to the Queen's Plate in Canada along with a gift of 50 guineas to the winner, still given by the monarch today. King Edward VII's horse Persimmon won the Derby in 1896 and Queen Elizabeth II is recognized as one of the world's greatest authorities on bloodlines and horse breeding.

> **Quickies**
> *Did you know ...*
> - that the Queen's Plate, held in Toronto since 1859, is the oldest continuously run horse race in North America?

> **Royal Plays**
> - *Victoria Regina* (Laurence Housman)
> - *Richard II* (Shakespeare)
> - *Victoria* (Kathleen Norris)
> - *Henry IV* (Shakespeare)
> - *Charles the King* (Maurice Colbourne)
> - *Henry V* (Shakespeare)
> - *Don Carlos* (Schiller)
> - *Henry VI* (Shakespeare)
> - *Mary Stuart* (Schiller)
> - *Richard III* (Shakespeare)
> - *Caesar and Cleopatra* (Shaw)
> - *Henry VIII* (Shakespeare)
> - *Ruy Blas* (Hugo)
> - *Antony and Cleopatra* (Shakespeare)
> - *A Man for All Seasons* (Robert Bolt)
> - *Macbeth* (Shakespeare)
> - *King Lear* (Shakespeare)
> - *Hamlet* (Shakespeare)

Who wrote the first story set in Canada?

Queen Marguerite of Navarre, sister of King François I, who sent Cartier to discover and settle Canada. The narrative was one Queen Marguerite wrote for her

Quickies

Did you know ...

- that George III's grandson, Sir Augustus d'Este, gave Kahkewaquonaby a steel peace pipe to use at the opening of Indian councils in Upper Canada?

Heptameron, an anthology of tales. It told the story of a couple marooned on a desert island in the Gulf of St. Lawrence.

What legacy did the Acadians receive from their king?

Louis XIII chose "Ave Maris Stella" ("Hail Star of the Sea") for them as their hymn. Today, Acadians still use it. It is a hymn to the Blessed Virgin Mary. The sea star of Mary is displayed on the Acadian flag.

Why is a first-class chef called a "cordon bleu"?

This term comes from our French kings. The *cordon bleu* was the blue ribbon worn by Knights of the Order of the Holy Spirit, the French equivalent of the Order of the Garter, founded in 1578 by King Henri III. *Cordon bleu* or "blue ribbon" came to be applied to wearers of the order themselves and then by extension to anyone of particular distinction. It was at first applied facetiously to special eminence in cooking but has now become a very serious designation for master chefs or even gifted amateur cooks. The story is told that King Louis XV so much appreciated the dinner given to him by Madame Du Barry that he wished to engage her cook for the Royal Household. He was informed that the cook was a woman and that she ought to have a reward worthy of her — nothing less than the cordon bleu. In English the term *blue ribbon* is derived in a way similar to *cordon bleu*. It comes from the blue ribbon of the Order of the Garter and was applied to anything deemed first class. This is why blue ribbons are awarded as prizes at shows, fairs, or exhibitions.

What is Canada's oldest corporation?

The Hudson's Bay Company created by King Charles II by royal charter

Canada's Royal Foundations

Institutions, cities, provinces, and corporations whose creation is closely identified with a monarch or member of the royal family.

Quebec City	Henri IV
Montreal	Louis XIV
Congregation de Notre Dame	Louis XIV
Hudson's Bay Company	Charles II/Prince Rupert
Charon Brothers Order	Louis XIV
Trois-Rivières	Louis XV
Grey Nuns	Louis XV
Halifax	George II
St. Paul's Church, Halifax	George II
St. John's Church, Lunenburg	George II
Toronto (York)	George III
Anglican Diocese of Quebec	George III
Christ Church Cathedral, Quebec	George III
McGill University (began 1801 as Royal Institution for the Advancement of Learning)	George III
St. Luke's Church, Placentia	William IV
New Brunswick	George III
Saint John	George III
University of King's College, Halifax	George III
Mohawk Chapels Royal, Tyendinaga and Brantford	George III
St. George's Church, Halifax	Duke of Kent
University of Toronto	George IV
University of Victoria College	William IV
University of Trinity College, Toronto	Victoria
Queen's University, Kingston	Victoria
National Gallery of Canada	Marquis of Lorne/Princess Louise
Royal Society of Canada	Marquis of Lorne/Princess Louise
Royal Canadian Academy	Marquis of Lorne/Princess Louise
Canadian Cancer Fund	George V

in 1670 is the oldest. Started originally to exploit the fur trade and explore the new world, it evolved into a retail giant in Canada, operating under the commercial name of The Bay.

Who wrote "God Save the Queen"?

No one knows. There are many theories about its origin. The inspiration for the words is the account of the anointing of King Solomon in the Jewish sacred writings. It states that all the people shouted "God save the King!" Some claim to have traced elements of the tune to a plainsong antiphon "They Anointed Solomon" used in medieval liturgy. Another theory is that Louis XIV's court musician Lulli was the composer. The story goes that when the king, in 1686, visited the academy for orphaned daughters of officers killed in the royal service, he was greeted by 300 voices singing "Grand dieu sauvez le roi! Grand dieu venger le roi! Vive le roi! Qu'a jamais glorieux Louis victorieux Voie ses ennemis toujours soumis! Vive le roi!" This version was believed in Quebec and by no less a person than Philippe-Joseph Aubert de Gaspé.

How long has "God Save the Queen" been used in Canada?

Almost exactly as long as in the United Kingdom. "God Save the King" became popular as a song to support the Hanoverian king, George II, during Bonnie Prince Charlie's Jacobite uprising of 1745. Soon afterwards the king's forces began to use the tune officially. Royal troops built Halifax as a garrison town in 1749 and were stationed there. They soon introduced "God Save the King" to the new world. Canada can truly claim joint ownership of the royal anthem. The first record of its being played before a member of the royal family in Canada was when George III's son Prince William arrived at Halifax in 1787. "God Save the Queen/King" has been rendered in Canada in English, French, Mohawk, Inuktituk, sign language, and other tongues.

Quickies

Did you know ...
- that the best known setting of the Royal Anthem in Canada was published in 1934 by Toronto musician and composer Sir Ernest Macmillan?

Royal Operettas and Musicals
- *Camelot*
- *The Student Prince*
- *The King and I*
- *Princess Ida*
- *Blondel*
- *The Mikado*
- *H.M.S. Pinafore*
- *The Grand Duke*
- *Pirates of Penzance*
- *Naughty Marietta*
- *The Gondoliers*

Who was the first king to eat a pineapple grown in England?

King Charles II was the first, in about 1670. By the 18th and 19th centuries, pineapples were being grown in heated greenhouses throughout England. They were prized by the rich and were a symbol for hospitality and luxury. They were so rare and expensive until the end of the 19th century that they were rented out as centrepieces and incorporated into architectural and design motifs.

How did the monarch butterfly get its name?

Settlers in the Thirteen Colonies were impressed by the beauty of the butterfly, and because its bright orange colour reminded them of their monarch, King William III of the House of Orange, they named the butterfly after him.

Ten of Canada's Greatest Royal Treasures

- Frère Luc's *La France apportant la Foi aux Indiens de la Nouvelle-France*: Ursulines Convent, Quebec City. The early Canadian painting depicts Queen Anne, the mother of Louis XIV, on the banks of the St. Lawrence River. Crowned, wearing rich robes of ermine and blue bespattered with gold fleurs-de-lys, Queen Anne incarnates the Royal House of Bourbon's mission to Christianize the aboriginal people of the new land, one of whom kneels before her with a mission station in the background. The French Crown was interested in the Natives as people, not just objects of exploitation.

- Mohawk Queen Anne Communion Plate: No object is more endowed with the pain, strife, fidelity, and adventure of Canadian history. Sent in 1711 by the Stuart Queen, Anne, to the Chiefs of the Iroquoian Confederacy after they had been received by Her Majesty at court, the double set of silver vessels by association, age, craftsmanship, and material substance is of incalculable value. When the Six Nations chose loyalty to the king at the American Revolution, they hid the silver and later brought it to Canada. Divided between the Mohawks of the Grand River and Tyendinaga in 1788, it is still in use.

- Marble Head of King George III: McCord Museum, McGill University, Montreal. The head is all that remains of a full statue of George III sent by the monarch as a gift to the people of Montreal in 1766. The statue was a visible, tangible token of George III's policy of conciliating his new French-Canadian subjects acquired when King Louis XV transferred Quebec to him, making him sovereign over all Canada. But royal generosity to the new French-speaking Catholic subjects angered the English merchants of Montreal. Thugs sympathetic to the American Revolution desecrated the statue in 1776, painting it black, decking it with a mock rosary of potatoes and a mitre on the head, and adding the sign "Behold the pope of Canada and the English fool." The rowdies later smashed the statue and dumped it in a well. Only the head was recovered, a lasting reminder of the wise royal policy that laid the groundwork for a bicultural Canada.

- Portrait of Queen Victoria: Senate of Canada, Ottawa. The Parliament Buildings in Montreal, then the seat of government, were destroyed by fire in 1849. This royal portrait was the only object rescued. A mob, angered that the governor general had given royal assent to a law compensating property loss resulting from the suppression of the Rebellion of 1837, started the fire. The governor general had, the previous year, introduced the principle that the life of a cabinet depends on its ability to command a parliamentary majority. Since the Rebellion Losses Bill had the support of the majority of the members of Parliament, His Excellency assented to it despite public hostility. The portrait, therefore, is more than a reminder of the agonies of Canada's constitutional evolution. It is the greatest tangible symbol and relic in existence of the introduction of responsible government in Canada.

- Duke of Kent's Town Clock, Halifax: Prince Edward the Duke of Kent lived in Halifax at the end of the 18th century as commander-in-chief of the Crown's forces in North America. The astute, hard-working Duke, son of

King George III and father of Queen Victoria, concluded that Haligonians were very unpunctual. He resolved to remedy this and, in 1803, after returning to the United Kingdom, he sent a large clock as a gift to the city, along with an expert to set it up. It was erected outdoors on Citadel Hill, overlooking historic Halifax Harbour. Since then, it has been a timepiece for busy citizens to set their watches by, and one of the city's most recognizable landmarks.

- City of Vancouver Mace: There are many maces — legislative, academic, and civic — in use in Canada. Vancouver's is unique. It is one of only two in the Commonwealth to bear the royal cipher E VIII R of King Edward VIII who reigned for only 325 days. The other Edward VIII mace belongs to Swindon, England.

- Queen Mary's Carpet: In 1942, during the Second World War, Queen Mary, widow of George V and the Queen Mother, began work on her famous carpet. She finished the gros point carpet measuring 3.1 x 2.1 metres in 1950. The work consists of 12 panels with designs adapted, on the queen's instructions, by the Royal School of Needlework from 18th century originals with colours chosen by Her Majesty, who did every stitch in the carpet herself. The Canadian women's patriotic organization IODE purchased it and presented it to the National Gallery of Canada, who clearly regard it as a great treasure, for it has not been seen by the public in decades.

- Portraits of the Four Mohawk Kings: During her Silver Jubilee celebrations in Ottawa, Queen Elizabeth II unveiled these paintings of the Iroquoian chiefs at the National Archives. The portraits, made by Jan Verlet at the time of the kings' visit to Queen Anne, hung for three centuries at Kensington Palace. Recognizing their importance as a part of Canadian heritage, the queen ensured them a permanent home in her Canadian realm.

- Queen's Beasts: Canadian Museum of Civilization, Ottawa. Ten heraldic plaster cast statues, 1.83 metres in height, created by James Woodford, RA, for the coronation of Elizabeth II in 1953. Several sets were made for use in the Commonwealth. One set stood in front of the temporary annex to Westminster Abbey. Originally only partially coloured, the Beasts, associated with figures of the royal line in the Middle Ages, where the roots of Canada's Parliament and system of law are found, were fully painted for the centenary of Confederation in 1967. Though on display at the museum, you have to ask to see them.

- Royal Arms of King George I: Trinity Church, Saint John. A beautiful polychrome woodcarving of 1714 set inside the great west doors of the church. The arms originally hung in the council chambers of the old State House of the Commonwealth of Massachusetts in Boston. When the Loyalists were evacuated from Boston, two Harvard graduates, Edward Winslow and Ward Chipman, took the royal arms with them. From Halifax they were sent to the new city of Saint John. Writing of the lion and unicorn supporters of the arms, Colonel Winslow noted they too had "run away when the others did, have suffered and are of course Refugees, and have a claim for residence at New Brunswick." The arms are an enduring reminder of how the Loyalists brought to Canada belief in fidelity, rule of law, and *evolution* rather than *revolution*.

Who was perhaps the most anti-intellectual monarch?

George I is a contender for the distinction. "I hate all Boets and Bainters" he once declared in his thick German accent. But not musicians — the king loved music and the opera and was a patron of the great composer George Frederick Handel, whose famous *Water Music* was written for George I's birthday.

Monarchs in Song *Anthems*	
"God Save the King/Queen"	Britain/Commonwealth, Norway
"God Bless the Prince of Wales"	Wales
"King Christian Stood by the Mast"	Denmark
"March of the Khedive"	Egypt
"God Preserve our Emperor"	Austria
"God Save our Noble Tsar"	Russia
"Partant pour la Syrie"	Second Empire France
"William of Nassau"	Netherlands
"Song of Brabant"	Belgium
"The Maple Leaf Forever"	Canada
"O Canada"	Canada
"Royal March"	Italy
"Hawai'I Pono'i" (by King Kalakaua)	Hawaii
"Long Live Our Shahinshah"	Iran / Persia
"Song of the King of the Tonga Islands"	Tonga
"Greetings to Our Neighbours!"	Monaco
"I, Servant of His Majesty"	Thailand
"May Our Lord Forever Reign"	Japan
"Royal Hymn"	Spain

Why does the audience always stand for one part of Handel's *Messiah*?

When King George II attended a performance of Handel's famous oratorio *Messiah*, he was so moved by the majesty of the "Hallelujah Chorus" that he suddenly rose to his feet and remained standing until it was finished. The rest of the audience of course stood when the king did. Audiences to this day have continued the practice begun by His Majesty King George II in tribute to Handel. George II was Handel's faithful patron and the composer wrote some of his finest works for the sovereign, works such as "Zadok the Priest" and the "Royal Fireworks Music."

Monarchs in Song *Folk Songs and Other Airs*	
"Queen Eleanor was a Sick Woman"	England
"No One Will Tell Me the Cause of My Sorrow" (by Richard I)	England
"Owre Kynge Went Forth to Normandy"	England
"Greensleeves" (by Henry VIII)	England
"The King's Hunt"	England
"Vive Henri Quatre"	France, Quebec
"When the King Enjoys His Own Again"	England, Scotland, Ireland
"Here's a Health Unto His Majesty"	England
"The Vicar of Bray"	Britain
"Chevaliers de la Table Ronde"	France, Quebec
"Vive le roi! Vive la reine!"	France, Quebec.
"Le Fils du Roi"	Quebec
"Will Ye No Come Back Again?"	Jacobite Scotland
"Charlie is My Darling"	Jacobite Scotland
"Wha'll be King but Charlie?	Jacobite Scotland
"O Richard, O mon roi"	France
"Queen's Prayer and Aloha Oe" (by Queen Lili'uokalani)	Hawaii

Why is a certain kind of pottery known as "Queen's Ware"?

In 1725, Thomas Astbury invented a cream-coloured, light-bodied earthenware which he called creamware. The great potter Josiah Wedgwood brought this creamware to a high degree of refinement during the 1760s, and it became famous throughout the world. In 1762, a set of creamware was presented to Queen Charlotte, consort of King George III. After Her Majesty accepted the set, Wedgwood changed the name of the ware to Queen's Ware, in honour of the queen's patronage, and it has been known as such ever since. Queen Charlotte knew that Wedgwood was going to name the ware in her honour but she expected that it would be called Charlotte Ware. The wily Wedgwood, however, knew that by calling it Queen's Ware, he would be able to present it to other female sovereigns and consorts as well. He soon did so to the Russian empress, Catherine the Great.

Quickies

Did you know ...

- that the first dictionary of the Huron, Algonkin, and Montagnais languages, compiled by the Recollet missionary Father Georges Le Baillif, was presented to King Louis XIII?

What is inscribed on the largest bell in the tower of Trinity Church, Saint John?

The words "In Memoriam the Loyalists 1783: Faithful alike to God and the King." The church also houses a royal coat of arms that Loyalists rescued from the city of Boston during the American Revolution.

What book did the Duke of Kent (father of Queen Victoria) help get published?

The Quebec topographer Joseph Bouchette's *A Topographical Description of Lower Canada* was encouraged by the Duke of Kent. Bouchette was one of the many French-Canadian friends the duke had acquired during his decade of residence in Canada in the late 18th century.

Royalty and Books	
David (traditionally author)	Psalms of David in the Bible
Solomon (traditionally author)	Books of Proverbs and Ecclesiastes in the Bible
Alfred the Great (translated)	Boethius' *De consolatione philosophiae*
Anna Comnena (author)	*The Alexiad*
James I (of Scotland, author)	*The Kingis Quair*
Maximilian I (author)	*Memoirs*
Henry VIII (author)	*Defence of the Seven Sacraments*
Edward VI (influenced)	*Book of Common Prayer* 1552
Henri II (dedicated to)	André Thevet's *Cosmographie universelle*
Elizabeth I (translated)	Queen Marguerite's *Le Miroir de l'âme pécheresse*
James I (inspired)	Authorized (King James) version of the Bible (author) *Basilikon Doron*
Charles I (author)	*Eikon Basilike*
Louis XIV (author)	*Mémoires et Réflexions*
Louis XIV (dedicated to)	Hennepin's *Description de la Louisiane*
Frederick II "the Great" (author)	*Histoire de Mon Temps, Art de la Guerre, Historie de Brandebourg, Histoire de la Guerre de Sept Ans*
Catherine II the Great (author)	*Memoirs*
George IV (dedicated to)	Jane Austen's *Emma*
Victoria (author)	*Leaves from the Journal of Our Life in the Highlands* (translated into many languages including Gujurati for India)
Marie (author)	*The Country that I Love*
Edward VIII (author)	*A King's Story*
Frederica (author)	*A Measure of Understanding*
Muhammad Reza Shah (author)	*Answer to History*

What celebrated Canadian author was unsuccessful in dedicating a book to the king?

Major John Richardson, the first Canadian novelist, asked permission to dedicate *The Canadian Brothers; or, The Prophecy Fulfilled: A Tale of the Late American War* about the War of 1812 to King William IV. His Majesty consented, but before Richardson was able to get the work published, the king died.

An explorer of Canada dedicated books to two monarchs. Who were they?

They were King Louis XIV and King William III. The interesting feature is that each was the head of one of the two rival royal houses then exercising sovereignty over Canada. The explorer was Joseph Hennepin, an energetic, adventurous but mercurial Recollet priest, who accompanied La Salle in 1678 via Niagara and Detroit to Michilimackinac and then by Lake Michigan and the Illinois River to the upper Mississippi region. Hennepin dedicated his *Descriptions de la Louisiane* about his discoveries and his life with the Sioux, who captured his party, to Louis XIV in 1683. He experienced a sudden fall from favour with Louis XIV, however, and his 1697 account *Nouvelle Découverte d'un très grand Pays* was dedicated to King William III who protected him in Holland. Fortunately William III had just made peace with his foe, Louis XIV, so such a dedication could not be called treason.

How did the Christmas tree come to be a regular part of Christmas festivities in Canada?

Prince Albert introduced the Christmas tree for Christmas festivities at Windsor Castle. It had been a much-loved part of Christmas when he was a child in Germany. From about 1848, the custom of the Christmas tree began to grow in popularity among Queen Victoria's subjects in many parts of the world, particularly after a print of the royal family and their Christmas tree appeared in the *Illustrated London News*. The royal family's example has been followed ever since.

How was use of the tartan revived?

Before 1747, the tartan was almost universally worn by Highland Scots. Following the attempt by the Stuarts to regain their throne in 1745, however, the tartan was proscribed by an "Act for the Abolition of Highland Dress and Tartan." By the early 19th century only a few people, regarded as somewhat eccentric, maintained the dress. But when Queen Victoria and Prince Albert made their residence at Balmoral Castle in 1847, the queen and her sons set a new fashion for wearing the tartan, and it was given a new lease on life. Since then, it has continued to be worn by Scots and those of Scottish ancestry or connection everywhere.

What medical innovation did Queen Victoria popularize?

Queen Victoria received chloroform to ease the pain when delivering her two youngest children, Prince Leopold in 1853 and Princess Beatrice in 1857. The royal example led to doctors and patients embracing the practice that subsequently became the normal procedure for childbirth.

> **Quickies**
> *Did you know ...*
> * that the Duke of Kent (father of Queen Victoria) was one of the earliest patrons of the theatre in Nova Scotia?

Of which Canadian-born singer did Queen Victoria become friend and patron?

Of the diva Madame Albani, a French-Canadian soprano, Queen Victoria wrote, "She is my Canadian subject, an excellent person, known to me, a splendid artiste, and I have taken much interest in her." The queen gave her numerous gifts and the Golden Jubilee Medal.

Which artist painted Queen Victoria and put himself in the picture?

Frederic Bell-Smith of Toronto, in his canvas "The Artist Painting Queen Victoria," now in the National Gallery of Canada. The queen sat for the artist, a high mark of esteem on her part. The Bell-Smith painting also includes Princess Louise.

How did the dessert cherries jubilee get its name?

The great French-born chef Georges Auguste Escoffier (1846–1935) created the dessert known as cherries jubilee in honour of the Golden Jubilee of Her Majesty Queen Victoria, which was celebrated in 1887. Escoffier was known as "the king of chefs and the chef of kings," and Queen Victoria's grandson, the Emperor Wilhelm II, once told him, "I am the emperor of Germany but you are the emperor of chefs."

Quickies

Did you know ...

- that a local anonymous donor gave the life-size statue inscribed "George VI. King of Canada 1936–1952. A Very Gallant Gentleman" at Niagara Falls, Ontario?

How did the queen's birthday become a national holiday in Canada?

It was in reaction to the Annexation Manifesto of 1849. Already a public holiday in the Province of Canada since 1845, the sovereign's birthday was boosted to a major celebration four years later. The citizens of Toronto, "the Queen City," determined to show their opposition to the idea of annexation to the United States, promoted by the manifesto signed by English-speaking Montrealers that year, decided to celebrate Queen

Victoria's birthday in a big way. Their style of celebration spread across the country.

What is the origin of the familiar Canadian jingle about the queen's birthday?

One year, a rumour that trustees were not going to give school-goers a holiday on May 24 caused discontent. In the country's first student protest, children showed their displeasure by chanting the rhyme "The twenty-fourth of May / is the queen's birthday / If you don't give us a holiday / we'll all run away." Spoilsport trustees quickly backed down.

What is one of the strangest ways the queen's birthday is marked in Canada?

The holiday is marked by the 21-anvil salute at New Westminster, British Columbia. As a garrison town, New Westminster had a 21-gun salute fired by the military on the sovereign's birthday. When the military left, the Hyack — the name is Chinook for "Hurry up!" — Volunteer Fire Department took over the practice. But there were no cannon on hand. Undaunted, the inventive fire brigade hit on placing gunpowder between two anvils, the top one upturned, and igniting the charge. The result was the "anvil salute" and ever since it has been fired at noon on Victoria Day. Crowning a local May Queen is also part of the yearly festival.

What personal possession of Queen Victoria's is at the Maritime Museum of the Atlantic?

The museum is home to the beautiful white barge presented to Queen

Victoria on her Golden Jubilee in 1887. Queen Elizabeth II gave the barge, whose keel is made of Canadian elm, to Canada in 1959 and it was transferred to the museum in 1981.

Which French-Canadian sculptor designed statues of two sovereigns?

Louis Philippe Hébert. He created the statue of Edward VII, *Hommages des Canadiens au roi pacificateur*, for Place du Canada in Montreal and the Queen Victoria Memorial on Parliament Hill in Ottawa.

In what musical comedy are there joint kings?

The Gondoliers by Gilbert and Sullivan. One of two brothers is the rightful King of Barataria but it is not known which. Meanwhile they reign jointly as "the King." They sing together "Rising Early in the Morning" about the functions of a constitutional monarch.

A fictional emperor of Japan is a somewhat grim character in which operetta?

The Mikado, one of the Savoy operas by Gilbert and Sullivan, features the fictional emperor of the show title. With ponderous dignity he sings "In a fatherly kind of way / I govern each tribe and sect / All cheerfully own my sway, I'm the Emperor of Japan."

Monarchs in Prose and Epic Poetry	
Priam, Menelaus, Agamemnon, and Nestor	Homer's *Iliad*
Ulysses	Homer's *Odyssey*
Dido and Aeneas	Virgil's *Aeneid*
Hrothgar	*Beowulf*
Charlemagne	*The Song of Roland*
Cambuscan	Chaucer's *Canterbury Tales*
Arthur	*The Mabinogian*
Arthur	Mallory's *Morte d'Arthur*
Tancred, Carlo, Pietro and Saladin	Boccaccio's *Decameron*
Shahryar	*The Arabian Nights*
Charlemagne	Ariosto's *Orlando Furioso*
Gloriana (Elizabeth I)	Spenser's *Faerie Queen*
Oberon and Titania	Shakespeare's *Midsummer Night's Dream*
Richard I "the Lion Heart"	Scott's *Ivanhoe*
Rudolf V, Flavia	Hope's *Prisoner of Zenda*
Yetive	McCutcheon's *Graustark*
Dolores	Jerrold's *Storm Over Europe*
John	Buchan's *House of the Four Winds*
Aragorn II	Tolkien's *Lord of the Rings*

Why is the bottom button of a gentleman's waistcoat always left undone?

This fashion originated with King Edward VII. As Prince of Wales he began to grow more portly when he entered middle age. He started leaving his bottom button undone to accommodate his girth, then decided it looked elegant to do so. Soon men, regardless of their personal shape, began to copy the prince's style and no gentleman wishing to look fashionable has done that button up since.

Who invented the dinner jacket (or tuxedo)?

The dinner jacket was invented to provide a less formal evening wear than white tie and tails, the 19th century gala dress for men. The originator was King Edward VII. As Prince of Wales he made the dinner jacket not only acceptable but fashionable for certain occasions. It was on his voyage to India in 1875 that he adopted a short, dark blue jacket with silk facings, worn with a bow tie and black trousers. Because the dinner jacket is called the "tuxedo" in the United States, some people think that it was invented by an American. The American name came about because in 1886 James Brown Potter, an American acquaintance of the Prince of Wales, stayed with the prince in London and the prince ordered his Savile Row tailor to make Potter one of the new dinner jackets. Potter then introduced the prince's fashion creation at Tuxedo Park, a resort in New York State, when he returned to the United States.

Why was the first pizza created?

While pita bread, the origins of pizza, was known for centuries, the classic pizza of Naples, as we know it, was created by the baker Raffaele Esposito in 1889 to celebrate the birthday of Queen Margherita of Italy at the request of her husband King Umberto I. Pizza Margherita features mozzarella cheese (white), tomatoes (red) and basil leaves (green), which are the colours of the House of Savoy and Italy.

What is King Oscar?

It is a an appetizer in Norwegian cuisine consisting of a buttered bread slice, mayonnaise, sliced cucumbers, and shrimps, and named after Oscar II, king of Sweden and Norway.

When was the earliest known hockey game played at Buckingham Palace?

In 1895 the five sons of Lord Stanley, who had been governor general of Canada and donated the Stanley Cup to hockey, organized a game on the frozen pond in the grounds of Buckingham Palace against a team from the palace, which included the Prince of Wales (later King Edward VII) and the Duke of York (later King George V).

What is the Prince of Wales Trophy in hockey?

The trophy was donated in 1924 by Prince Edward, Prince of Wales, to the National Hockey League, originally for its championship. When the NHL became the only league to compete for the Stanley Cup, which had been donated for the championship of Canada by Lord Stanley when he was governor general, the Prince of Wales Trophy was awarded for subordinate champions in the league. It is currently awarded to the playoff champions of the Eastern Conference of the NHL.

> **Quickies**
>
> *Did you know …*
>
> • that children in early York (Toronto) used a counting-out rhyme about the controversial Queen Caroline, estranged wife of George IV? It went: "Queen, Queen Caroline / Washed her face in turpentine / Turpentine made it shine / Queen, Queen Caroline."

When did Queen Elizabeth II attend her first hockey game?

The queen attended a hockey game in Montreal in 1959, at which the famous Maurice "Rocket" Richard presented to her the puck with which he scored his 500th goal.

Royal Nursery Rhymes, Verse, Ballads, Poems, and Carols	
"Old King Cole"	Britain
"Queen Eleanor's Confession"	England
"Kingdoms are but cares" (by Henry VI)	England
"The King of France went up the hill."	England
"Green Groweth the Holly" (by Henry VIII)	England
"The Queen of Hearts"	England
"When I was young and fair" (by Elizabeth I)	England
"Please to remember the fifth of November"	England
"Mark how the blushful morn in vain" (by Charles I)	England
"Close thine eyes and sleep secure" (by Charles I)	England
"Good King Wenceslaus"	England
"I'm the king of the castle!"	England
"Humpty Dumpty"	England
"Belshazzar from the banquet turn"	England
"Morte D'Arthur" (Tennyson)	Britain/Commonwealth
"Ballad to an Absent Friend" (by prince consort)	Britain/Commonwealth
"Pretty Baby" (by prince consort)	Britain/Commonwealth
"The Island Rose"	Hawaii/Scotland

Who was the only Commonwealth composer outside the United Kingdom to write music for Elizabeth II's coronation?

Healey Willan, dean of Canadian composers, provided the fourth of the five homage anthems for the coronation. It was "O Lord, Our Governor" and drew on Psalms 8, 84, 17, 61, 21, and 20. This was the music played while the Duke of Edinburgh, the other royal dukes, and the representative peers pledged their loyalty to the queen after her enthronement.

Swans traditionally are regarded as the property of the Crown. Does the Crown have a right to other creatures?

Sturgeon, by ancient right, belong to the Crown too. At the time of Queen Elizabeth II's cross-country tour in 1959, a Nova Scotia trawler caught a 350-pound one. Knowing about this royal right, the owners asked permission to send it to the queen at Rideau Hall where Her Majesty was in residence. It was duly inspected in the kitchen by the queen.

Which Canadian museum has footwear worn by Prince Philip?

The Bata Shoe Museum in Toronto contains footwear of the prince in its extensive collection. The museum also has in its collection a pair of 19th-century Burmese royal shoes which were traditionally worn by the Buddhist kings of what is now known as Myanmar. The shoes are believed to date to the last Burmese dynasty, the Konbang dynasty, which lasted from 1755 to 1885.

Crowns in Film

- *Anne of the Thousand Days*
- *The Prisoner of Zenda*
- *The Private Lives of Elizabeth and Essex*
- *The Student Prince*
- *Ivanhoe*
- *The Adventures of Robin Hood*
- *The Lord of the Rings*
- *55 Days at Peking*
- *The Lion in Winter*
- *Nicholas and Alexandra*
- *Anna and the King of Siam*
- *The Swan*
- *The Madness of King George*
- *Victoria the Great*
- *A Man for All Seasons*
- *Sixty Glorious Years*
- *Bonnie Prince Charlie*
- *Mary, Queen of Scots*
- *Mary of Scotland*
- *The Queen*
- *The Virgin Queen*
- *King Richard and the Crusaders*
- *The Mouse that Roared*
- *The Emperor Waltz*
- *The Private Life of Henry VIII*
- *The Last Emperor*
- *Throne of Blood*
- *Mayerling*
- *Catherine the Great*
- *Alexander Nevsky*
- *Ivan the Terrible*
- *Hamlet*
- *Henry V*

What modern pop musical is unapologetically royalist?

Tim Rice and Stephen Oliver's *Blondel*. (Blondel was the troubadour who according to tradition discovered where Richard I "the Lion

127

Heart" was imprisoned.) Its theme song runs "I'm a monarchist / Loyal through and through / Talk of presidents gives offence / Only kings will do" et cetera.

canada's
royal ties

Which members of the royal family have been sworn of the Canadian Privy Council?

King Edward VIII was made a member of His Majesty's Privy Council for Canada when Prince of Wales in 1927. His Royal Highness the Duke of Edinburgh was admitted in 1957. The latter occurred during the 1957 stay in Ottawa by the queen and the duke, during Queen Elizabeth II's first tour in Canada as monarch. A meeting of the Queen's Privy Council in the presence of the queen was arranged by Prime Minister John Diefenbaker, at which the duke was admitted to the council.

Where did King Edward VIII consider living once he abdicated?

At the time of the abdication, the king talked seriously of taking up permanent residence at the EP Ranch, the property he purchased in 1919 at High River, Alberta. As it happened, he went to France instead. It is hard to imagine Wallis Simpson taking easily to the rustication of an Alberta rancher's wife.

On what foreign tour did Elizabeth II wear her famous maple leaf dress?

The maple leaf dress was created for the 1959 tour when Her Majesty opened the St. Lawrence Seaway. It was subsequently worn on her state visit to Italy in 1961.

Which member of the royal family advanced 18th century exploration of Canada?

When Louis XV came to the throne as a child, his cousin Prince Philippe, Duke of Orleans, became regent for him from 1715 until he came of age in 1723. (In French monarchical law kings were legally of age at 13.) The regent was a strange mixture of brilliance and degeneracy, a minor poet and patron of the arts, a liberal but very cynical freethinker, a man of intellectual distinction. Philippe almost succeeded in overturning the restrictions Louis XIV had placed on the regency in his will. "I have been proclaimed regent and during the minority I must have a king's authority," Philippe declared. The regency was a time of artistic flair but economic disaster. Philippe was keenly interested in the question of the existence of a western sea. This fascination led him as regent to commission Father Pierre-François-Xavier de Charlevoix to seek a route to this sea through the Canadian hinterland. Charlevoix's expedition took place in 1720–1722. He explored northern Ontario and sailed down the Mississippi River to New Orleans. Not only did this expedition open up the interior of Canada, it also led Charlevoix to publish in 1744 his *Histoire et Description générale de la Nouvelle France avec le journal historique d'un Voyage fait par Order du Roi dans l'Amérique septentrionale* which is the first general history of Canada ever written. Charlevoix dedicated this work to Jean-Marie de Bourbon, grandson of the Duke du Maine, Louis XIV's legitimized son by Madame de Montespan. Before the regent died in 1723, he also appointed François Gendron, the first doctor in Ontario, as his personal physician.

> **Quickies**
> *Did you know ...*
> * that the famous Princes' Gates at Exhibition Place in Toronto are named after Prince Edward, Prince of Wales (later King Edward VIII), and his brother Prince George, Duke of Kent (killed in the Second World War)?

Which two illegitimate daughters of William IV lived in Canada?

The king's second daughter, Mary FitzClarence, whose husband, General Charles Richard Fox, was stationed in Nova Scotia as commanding officer of the 34th Regiment in the 1830s, and his youngest daughter, Amelia FitzClarence, who married Viscount Falkland, Governor of Nova Scotia, 1840–1846.

What was the sole official external engagement Edward VIII carried out as king?

King Edward VIII reigned for less than one year. He did not undertake any foreign tours in that time. However, he did preside at the unveiling of the great Canadian Memorial at Vimy Ridge in France. The land was given to Canada in perpetuity but remains under the sovereignty of France, so the king's attendance was both a stay in Canada and a visit to France.

What Canadian mountain is a lasting mark of affection for an afflicted member of the British royal family?

Mount Prince John, British Columbia, located in the Royal Group east of Invermere, was named for the epileptic youngest son of King George V and Queen Mary. Prince John, when diagnosed as epileptic, lived apart from his family at Windsor, cared for by his devoted Nanny, Mrs. Lalla Bill. He died at the age of 14.

How did the Sikhs first come to Canada?

A contingent from India attended the Diamond Jubilee celebrations of Queen Victoria in London in 1897. While there, they met members of the North West Mounted Police (now the RCMP) who suggested they return home via Canada. They did. That led to Sikhs settling in British Columbia.

What "royal" gift did the French Republic give Canada in 1931?

It replaced the bust of King Louis XIV that originally stood in Place Royale, Quebec City, but disappeared at the conquest, with a new one, a copy of the famous sculpture by Bernini.

Of which governor general of Canada is Prince William of Wales a descendant?

Charles Lennox, fourth Duke of Richmond, was appointed governor general in 1818, but after just a year in office, died after being bitten by a fox. The descent is through Prince William's mother Diana, the late Princess of Wales. The Duke of Richmond, a professional soldier, fought at least two duels with the Duke of York, George III's second son. His wife, the Duchess of Richmond, gave the celebrated Waterloo Ball on the eve of the battle that ended the career of Napoleon I.

Who are Canada's greatest monarchs and why?

Of Canada's 33 monarchs, 15 were outstanding for what they did for the country. Henry VII and François I got Canada off to its start by sending Giovanni Caboto and Jacques Cartier to make their discoveries and initial contact with the Native peoples. Elizabeth I continued exploration, concentrating on the Northwest Passage and Newfoundland. Henri IV made engaging in the fur trade contingent of settlement, showing the country was not just for exploitation. James I, "the wisest fool (i.e. jester) in Christendom," laid the foundations of the British Empire from which Canada derived its law and parliamentary government. Charles I founded the Baronets of Nova Scotia to undertake settlement and granted the Western Charter, the basis of Newfoundland law for a century and a half. Louis XIII chartered the Company of One Hundred Associates, charged with bringing in 300 settlers a year. Louis XIV created Quebec, a royal province, thereby assuring a lasting francophone

> **Five Longest Reigns in Canadian History (1497-present)**
> - King Louis XIV (May 14, 1643–September 1, 1715) 72 years, 3 months, 18 days
> - Queen Victoria (June 20, 1837–January 22, 1901) 63 years, 7 months, 2 days
> - King George III (October 25, 1760–January 29, 1820) 59 years, 3 months, 4 days
> - Queen Elizabeth II (February 6, 1952–present) 57 years as of February 6, 2009 and counting
> - King Louis XV (September 1, 1715–February 10, 1763 [Treaty of Paris]) 47 years, 5 months, 9 days

133

community in North America. Charles II, by royal charter, created the Hudson's Bay Company, the most dynamic agent of Canadian history and one of the world's oldest corporations. James II, second governor of the Hudson's Bay Company, obtained the agreement of his brother Charles II that the company's charter applied not just to the Hudson Bay coastline but to the interior also, a crucial development in Canada's coming to acquire its northwestern terrain. Queen Anne laid the foundations of a lasting relationship between Crown and native peoples. George III united sovereignty over all Canada in his Crown and funded Loyalist settlement that created a viable English Canada. Victoria, "the Mother of Confederation," was the common bond that allowed the provinces to overcome local interest and unite as one Dominion. George V enacted the Statute of Westminster, giving Canada legal independence. George VI made the greatest of the royal tours, one that boosted national unity as Canada emerged from the Depression and entered the Second World War.

> **Quickies**
> *Did you know ...*
> • that François Gendron, a Jesuit who spent seven years in Huronia, treated Louis XIV's mother Queen Anne for cancer in 1666 and became physician to the regent (Duke of Orleans) for Louis XV?

What gift was sent to Louis XIV from Canada when he was born?

When they learned of the birth of the king's son, the aboriginals of New France sent the baby prince, who would become one of the greatest monarchs in history, a beaded papoose outfit.

What royal monument was paid for by children?

The Children's Memorial to Queen Victoria in Vancouver. Schoolchildren of the city donated pennies to cover the cost. The 1.8-metre-high granite memorial is located in Stanley Park, and was erected in 1905.

What rent was the reigning monarch entitled to from the Hudson's Bay Company?

Two elk heads and two black beaver pelts under the Royal Charter of Charles II. The tribute was paid four times on Canadian soil. It was first received in 1927 by the Prince of Wales (Edward VIII) on behalf of George V. King George VI was the first monarch to receive it in person, in 1939. Queen Elizabeth II accepted it in 1959 and 1970. The second time, in keeping with growing sensitivity to environmentalism, the rent took the form of live beavers. (The queen gave them to the Winnipeg Zoo.) In 1970 the Hudson's Bay Company had the Royal Charter amended to eliminate the rent. Killed! A great symbolic link to Canada's historic roots.

Five Shortest Reigns in Canadian History (1497-present)

- King Edward VIII (January 20, 1936–December 11, 1936 [abdicated]) — 10 months, 21 days
- King Francois II (July 10, 1559–December 5, 1560) — 1 year, 4 months, 25 days
- King James II (February 6, 1685–February 13, 1689 [overthrown]) — 4 years, 7 days
- Queen Mary I (July 6, 1553–November 17, 1558) 5 years, 4 months, 11 days
- Queen Mary II (February 13, 1689–December 28, 1694) 5 years, 10 months, 15 days

What native Canadian animal did Prince Philip save?

His Royal Highness is credited with saving the wood bison, commonly called the buffalo, in Canada. Prince Philip has been an advocate of green practice in Canada since the early 1950s, when he made his first solo coast to coast tour of the country, and has never ceased raising public awareness in this regard. "Conservation," he told the Canadian Audubon Society in 1967, "is really a case of now or never....Wildlife, whether in the shape of birds, animals, fish, or plants, is being threatened or eroded as never before in history. If we don't get the answer right now, there won't be a second chance."

What royal name did Sir George Étienne Cartier, chief French Canadian architect of Confederation, give his daughter?

He called one of his three daughters Reine Victoria Cartier — that is, Queen Victoria Cartier. Cartier himself received the name George, after King George III, from his parents. That is why George is spelled without the *s* which it would otherwise have in French.

How did Princess Louise sum up the position of governor general of Canada?

Writing from Rideau Hall to her youngest brother, Prince Leopold, the Duke of Albany, Her Royal Highness said: "I think it possible you may come here one day. Canada is so loyal, so interesting, and with such a marvelous future that it really seems as if the governor generalship should always be filled by a member of our family." As an intelligent perceptive woman, the princess had grasped the weakness in the position. Unless the holder was a member of the royal family, the governor generalcy would not realize its full potential as a viceregal office. It is the royal connection that takes it from an administrative to a representational role.

What was the strangest royal incident at Rideau Hall?

Official home of Canada's sovereign and her governors general, Government House in Ottawa has seen its share of royal dramas. The injured Princess Louise was brought home there after her serious sleigh accident. Princess Louise Margaret, the ailing Duchess of Connaught, chatelaine 1911 to 1916, agonized silently within its walls at the spectacle of her son fighting on the Allied side and her brother and nephew on the German side in the First World War. At Rideau Hall years later her grandson, the sad Prince Alastair, second Duke of Connaught, died prematurely from winter exposure.

Quotes from Canada's Kings and Queens?

- Edward VI: Noted in his diary that the French ambassador complained to him that the emperor "stayed certain ships French going a-fishing to the Newfoundland."
- Henri IV: Having to renounce Protestantism for Catholicism to ascend the throne: "Paris is worth a mass."
- Elizabeth I: In a speech to her judges: "Have a care over my people!"
- James I: His thoughts on smoking: "A custom loathsome to the eye, hateful to the Nose, harmefull to the braine, dangerous to the Lungs, and the black stinking fume thereof, nearest resembling the horrible Stigian smoke of the pit that is bottomlesse."
- Charles I: On the scaffold: "Remember!"
- Charles II: Defining constitutional monarchy: "My words are my own, and my actions are my ministers'."
- Louis XIV: *"L'État c'est moi!"* ("I am the State!")
- William III: "Every bullet has its billet."
- Louis XV: Appalled by the cost of building the Fortress of Louisbourg in Cape Breton: "One morning I expect to look out of my window at Versailles and see the towers of Louisbourg looming on the horizon."
- Anne: Touching for the King's Evil (scrofula): "May God heal you, the Queen touches you."
- George II: On hearing that people said General James Wolfe was mad: "If he is mad, then I wish he would bite some of my other generals."
- George III: To the first French-Canadian lady received at Court: "Madame, if all Canadian women resemble you, I have indeed made a fine conquest."
- William IV: On Halifax: "A very gay and lively place full of women, and those of the most obliging kind."
- Victoria: Discovering she would one day become queen: "I will be good."
- Edward VII: "We are all Socialists now-a-days."
- George V:On his deathbed: "How is the Empire?"
- Edward VIII: While abdicating: "I have found it impossible to carry the heavy burden of responsibility and to discharge my duties as King as I would wish to do without the help and support of the woman I love."
- George VI: To Parliament in Ottawa: "It is my earnest hope that my present visit may give my Canadian people a deeper conception of their unity as a nation … May the blessing of Divine Providence rest upon your labours and upon my realm of Canada."
- Elizabeth II: Leaving California for British Columbia: "I'm going home to Canada tomorrow."

But most resembling a melodramatic scene from a Ruritainian novel was the experience of another princess, Princess Marie Louise. In 1900, Her Serene Highness was staying at Rideau Hall before beginning a private train journey prescribed by her doctor to Vancouver through the Rockies. Wed some years before to Prince Aribert of Anhalt, and unhappy in her childless marriage, Princess Marie Louise had suffered a breakdown in health. Her luggage had already been stowed on the westbound train and she was ready to depart from Government House when the governor general appeared with a telegram from her father-in-law, Frederick I, Duke of Anhalt. The telegram sent *en clair* (readable by everyone whose hands it passed through) was a peremptory order for Princess Marie Louise to return to Germany.

Shocked, the princess was struggling with the temptation to ignore the command when another telegram arrived, this one from her grandmother, Queen Victoria. It was in code and said: "Tell my granddaughter to come home to me. V.R." Only when she returned to Cumberland Lodge, her parents' home at Windsor Castle, did Marie Louise discover the reason for the unexpected interruption of her tour at Government House. Without any consultation, her father-in-law had used his sovereign power as reigning prince of Anhalt to annul her marriage to his son. Neither Prince Aribert nor Princess Marie Louise ever re-married.

What was Queen Victoria's personal contribution to the preservation of old Quebec?

She paid for the erection of a new gate in the walls of the ancient city. It was called the Kent Gate after her father who lived several years in the city.

With which governor's wife did Prince William (William IV) have a love affair?

The beautiful Frances, Lady Wentworth, wife of Sir John Wentworth, Governor of Nova Scotia and formerly Royal Governor of Vermont.

For whom were the first 13 townships surveyed in Ontario (Upper Canada) named?

They were named by Lord Dorchester, the governor, for King George III, Queen Charlotte, and 11 of their children. The townships were Adolphustown, Augusta, Charlottenburgh, Cornwall, Edwardsburgh, Elizabethtown, Ernestown, Fredericksburgh, Kingston, Marysburgh, Matilda, Osnabruck, and Williamsburgh. They were known as the "Royal Townships." Ameliasburgh and Sophiasburgh were added later for the monarchs' two youngest children.

Which physician to King Louis XIV was a Canadian pioneer?

Michel Sarrazin came to Canada in 1685, received a Quebec fief, became surgeon-major to the royal troops and a member of the Superior Council and was a correspondent of the Academy of Science on Canadian flora and fauna.

What was Canada's gift to Queen Victoria for her Diamond Jubilee?

Creation of the famed Victorian Order of Nurses (VON) was arranged by Lady Aberdeen, wife of the governor general as Canada's gift to mark the 60th anniversary of the queen's reign.

Who presided at Quebec City's 300th birthday celebrations in 1908?

The Prince of Wales, later King George V, presided at the tercentenary and reviewed the great military pageant and parade that took place on the Plains of Abraham.

What prank did Prince Albert play in Canada in 1913?

When Canadian news reporters swarmed aboard HMS *Cumberland* on which Prince Albert, future King George VI, was serving, the young prince got a fellow midshipman to take his place and give an interview. The imaginative stand-in said the prince was treated the same as all the others on board ship except that he always wore a bowler hat on Sundays.

Quickies

Did you know ...

- that Canada's famous Polish engineer, Sir Casimir Gzowski, was personal aide de camp to Queen Victoria and did periods of service at Windsor Castle?

What was C.W. Jeffreys's quip on learning that King George V had made the mad Sam Hughes, Canadian Minister of Militia, a knight?

"*Le roi s'amuse!*" he exclaimed, or in translation "The king is having a bit of fun!"

Which king initiated German immigration to Canada?

George II. He was responsible for Germans establishing Lunenburg, Nova Scotia, in 1753 for settlers from Germany.

Which king personally settled a quarrel over the vacant Diocese of Quebec?

King Louis XV in 1727.

What was royal about Ontario's first blast furnace?

The first Ontario blast furnace, an air furnace to smelt ore in the Algoma region of northern Ontario, was the work of a partnership of three entrepreneurs. Two of them — Alexander Baxter and Alexander Henry — were businessmen on the scene and involved in the fur trade. The third partner in the enterprise was Prince William Henry, Duke of Gloucester, youngest and favourite brother of King George III. Under the Bourbon regime it had become known that Algoma was rich in copper and held out promise of other minerals. The partnership of Baxter, Henry, and the Duke of Gloucester built vessels on Lake Huron to promote mining.

Who were "the King's daughters"?

One of the challenges facing the young colony of New France was the lack of women to allow the population to grow. To solve this problem, young women were sent to Canada by King Louis XIV as brides for settlers and soldiers in the years 1654 to 1672. They are known to history as "the King's daughters."

What heroine did Louis XIV grant a pension to?

Madeleine Jarret de Verchères, heroine of the eight-day Iroquois siege of Verchères, Quebec, in 1692.

When the floundering settlement of Quebec appealed for help, what was the king's reply?

Pierre Boucher, emissary of the settlers, reported His Majesty's words: "I had the honour of speaking to the King, who questioned me about the state of the country, of which I gave him an accurate account, and His Majesty promised me that he would take it under his protection." The king was as good as his word and made Quebec a royal province. Soldiers, settlers, and money were poured into the province over the following years until it was established on a firm and lasting foundation.

Quickies

Did you know ...

- that George III's youngest son, the Duke of Sussex, was vice-president of the Society for Promoting Education and Industry among the Indians and Destitute Settlers in Canada?

Who presented the first Mohawk translation of the *Book of Common Prayer* to the Native people?

It was presented by King George III and Queen Charlotte.

Which Canadian factory worker produced a well-known book on George I's descendants?

Arnold McNaughton of Quebec. He spent 25 years researching, arranging, and publishing *The Book of Kings*. Enjoying the encouragement of Earl Mountbatten of Burma, McNaughton was appointed his personal genealogist, in which capacity he helped keep the famous Mountbatten *Relationship Tables* up to date.

Who named British Columbia?

Queen Victoria did, in 1858, the year the mainland was established as a province of the Crown separate from Vancouver Island. "New Vancouver, New Columbia, and New Georgia … do not appear on all maps" Her Majesty wrote at the end of June that year about the name of the new jurisdiction. "The only name which is given the whole territory in every map the Queen has consulted is 'Columbia,' but as there exists a Columbia in South America, and the citizens of the United States called their country also Columbia, at least in poetry, 'British Columbia' might be, in the Queen's opinion, the best name." Victoria also chose the name of the British Columbia city of New Westminster the following year.

What was the first organization that Queen Elizabeth II designated "royal" when she became monarch?

In 1952, the queen made the Winnipeg Ballet the "Royal Winnipeg Ballet."

Royal Consorts Since Confederation

- Queen Alexandra (1901–1910), wife of King Edward VII
- Queen Mary (1910–1936), wife of King George V
- Queen Elizabeth (1936–1952), wife of King George VI
- Prince Philip (1952–present), husband of Queen Elizabeth II

Who is the Queen Elizabeth Way in Ontario named after?

The first expressway built in Ontario, the Queen Elizabeth Way, was opened in 1939 by Queen Elizabeth, the consort of King George VI, after whom it was named.

Quickies

Did you know …

- that Prince Philip, Duke of Edinburgh, is second in seniority of membership in the Queen's Privy Council for Canada?

Why did King George VI and Queen Elizabeth arrive two days late to start the 1939 royal tour of Canada?

The *Empress of Australia*, bringing the king and queen to Canada, was stuck in an iceberg field in the North Atlantic for two days. The queen wrote to Queen Mary, "We very nearly hit a berg the day before yesterday, and the poor captain was nearly demented because some kind cheerful people kept on reminding him that it was about here that the *Titanic* was struck, and just about the same date!"

When was the first royal walkabout?

The word *walkabout* originated in Wellington, New Zealand, on the 1970 royal tour by Queen Elizabeth II and the Duke of Edinburgh, when they left their car and walked freely among the crowds. The first actual walkabout, though, occurred in Ottawa on the 1939 royal tour when King George VI and Queen Elizabeth spontaneously decided to break with the official plans during the unveiling of the War Memorial and mingled with the crowd of veterans.

Who was the first governor of the Hudson's Bay Company?

Prince Rupert of the Rhine, a first cousin of King Charles II and hero of the civil war against the Cromwellians was the first governor. Rupert's Land (the vast territory of the company) was named after him.

Which Canadian communities have won the Prince of Wales' architectural award?

The Town of Aurora in Ontario was the most recent (2008) recipient of the Prince of Wales' Prize for Municipal Heritage Leadership while the Municipality of Saint-Raymond de Portneuf, Quebec, was given an honourable mention. Other communities that have gained the prize for demonstrating a strong and sustained commitment to supporting their historic places have been Markham (2000), Victoria (2001), Saint John (2002), Quebec (2003), Perth (2004), Charlottetown (2005), Annapolis Royal (2006), and St. John's (2007). Since his youth, concern for architecture, the environment, and inner-city renewal has been a major theme of the Prince of Wales' public life. It led to the establishment of the Municipal Heritage Leadership Prize as part of the Heritage Canada Foundation's National Awards Program in 1999. To qualify, a local jurisdiction must have a record of supporting heritage preservation through regulation, policies, funding, and stewardship.

> **Quickies**
> *Did you know ...*
> • that the man who worked out the financial terms of the abdication settlement of King Edward VIII was the Canadian financier, Sir Edward Peacock, from Glengarry, Ontario?

When was "O Canada" first played?

Composed by Calixa Lavallée and Sir Basile Routhier at the request of the St. Jean Baptiste Society, it was first played at a concert before the Marquis of Lorne, Governor General of Canada and son-in-law of Queen Victoria, in Quebec City on June 24, 1880 (St. Jean Baptiste Day).

Why are there swans in the Rideau River in Ottawa?

The swans in Ottawa are royal swans, descendants of those given to the City of Ottawa in 1959 by Queen Elizabeth II on her royal tour that year.

Why was there no toast to King George VI at the official dinner at Rideau Hall during the 1939 royal tour?

Rideau Hall is the sovereign's home in Canada. Since the dinner was held at Rideau Hall, the king was the host, not a guest, so a toast to his health was not proposed.

Who was the first person outside the royal household to be told of the impending birth of Prince Andrew, Duke of York?

Queen Elizabeth II learned from her doctor that she was pregnant during the 1959 royal tour of Canada. Since she was in her Canadian realm, her Canadian prime minister took precedence over her British prime minister, so John Diefenbaker, prime minister of Canada was the first person informed and Harold Macmillan, prime minister of the United Kingdom was told later.

How did American president Harry Truman refer to Queen Elizabeth II on her 1951 visit to the United States?

Years Queen Elizabeth II Has Been to Canada

- 1951, 1953 (stop-over), 1957, 1959, 1963 (three stop-overs), 1964, 1967, 1970, 1971, 1973 (twice), 1974 (two stop-overs), 1976, 1977, 1978, 1982, 1983, 1984, 1985 (stop-over), 1986 (stop-over), 1987, 1990, 1991 (stop-over), 1992, 1994, 1997, 2002, 2005, 2007 (at Vimy Ridge)

In 1951, Princess Elizabeth undertook a major cross-country tour of Canada and then followed it with a short visit to the United States. As Canada is the closest neighbour of the U.S., and Elizabeth had arrived there from Canada, the American president officially greeted her as the "Canadian Princess."

Who were the Four Mohawk Kings?

In 1710, four Mohawk chiefs, Etow Oh Koam (Nicholas), Tee Yee Neem Ho Ga Row (Hendrick), Sa Ga Yeath Qua Pieth Tow (Brant), and No Nee Yeath Taw No Row (John) visited Queen Anne in England to cement the alliance between the Crown and the Mohawks. They were welcomed as the "four kings" and their trip achieved its purpose. Queen Anne sent a communion plate for the Mohawks back to North America, which was brought by them to Canada following the American Revolution, in which the Mohawks remained loyal to the Crown.

Quickies
Did you know ...
- that when Kahkewaquonaby or Sacred Feathers (the Reverend Peter Jones) was received by Queen Victoria in 1838 he was allowed to wear Mississauga garb and headdress as the aboriginal equivalent of court attire?

What did a waitress in a small Canadian town reportedly say to a royal duke?

Legend has it that she said, "Keep your fork Duke, there's pie coming," when she put his used fork back on the table as she removed the main course plate. The story may be true, but it has been told so many times about so many dukes and so many towns that it may well be apocryphal, combining Canadians' self image of small town informality, endearing familiarity with the royal family, and royal acceptance of Canadian quirks. While many people believe the encounter is about Prince Philip, Duke of Edinburgh, the first known appearance of the story predates the First World War, with Prince Arthur, Duke of Connaught and governor general of Canada, as the royal duke in question.

Quickies
Did you know ...
- that Queen Victoria told the aboriginal clergyman, the Reverend Henry Pahtaquahong Chase of Munceytown, Ontario, Ojibway President of the Indian Grand Council, quite bluntly that she wanted him to call his expected grandchild Victor in case of a boy or Victoria in case of a girl? It was a boy and Victor he became.

What writer gave a tongue-in-cheek account of George V's visit to Orillia?

Stephen Leacock, the internationally acclaimed Canadian humourist, in his comparison of Canada and England called *My Discovery of England*. In it he discussed the royal visit to Orillia as an example of the different attitudes of Canadians and English towards the Crown. After describing how the Orillians invited the (then) prince to an oyster supper, to play pool, to visit the new sewerage plant, and to cash a cheque at the Royal Bank, Leacock concludes that Canadians "understand Kings and Princes better than the English do" and "treat them in a far more human heart to heart fashion," adding that "[the English] have seen so much of the mere outside of ... kingship that they don't understand the heart of it as we do in Canada."

Six Significant Moments During Queen Elizabeth IIs Canadian Visits

- **1957** Her Majesty wore her shimmering jewel-embroidered Hartnell coronation dress, decorated with maple leaves and other floral emblems of her different Crowns, when she opened the first session of her 23rd Canadian Parliament in person and delivered the Speech from the Throne on October 14 in Ottawa.
- **1970** To mark the first trip to the Arctic by a reigning monarch, Queen Elizabeth II was presented with a narwhal tusk, similar to the one given to Queen Elizabeth I by the explorer Sir Martin Frobisher five centuries earlier. The tusk was subsequently placed on the Royal Yacht *Britannia*.
- **1976** As monarch of Canada, Elizabeth II opened the XXI Olympic Games in Montreal. She focused the world's attention on the event even more by unexpectedly bringing together the entire immediate royal family on Canadian soil for the first time during the games.
- **1982** When she signed the Proclamation patriating the Canadian Constitution on April 17 on Parliament Hill in Ottawa, Her Majesty transferred authority from herself as queen of the United Kingdom to herself as queen of Canada.
- **1997** Presiding at the celebration of the arrival of Giovanni Caboto's ship the *Matthew* in Newfoundland on June 24, 1497, the queen marked the beginning of royal authority in the "Kingdom of the North" — 500 years of monarchy in Canada.
- **2007** Vimy Ridge, site of the famous Canadian victory in the First World War, was given to Canada by France but remains under French sovereignty. When the queen visited the site to re-dedicate the Vimy Memorial on April 9, the visit was simultaneously a domestic tour and an international one for Her Majesty as queen of Canada.

the
crown
and the
commonwealth

Did Queen Victoria really say "We are not amused"?

She did. But her remark has been quoted out of context. This is what really happened. One day she overheard someone make a derogatory, off-colour remark about one of the ladies of her court. She reproved the speaker with the celebrated words, letting him know she did not find his ungentlemanly comment funny. Far from being humourless, the great queen had a keen sense of fun and liked to laugh. She did, however, think members of the royal family should avoid being photographed smiling for fear that the public would think them frivolous.

Which British/Commonwealth king had the most children?

King George III had 15 children of which 13 survived childhood. They were George (King George IV), Frederick (Duke of York), William (King William IV), Charlotte (Queen of Wurttemberg), Edward (Duke of Kent), Augusta, Elizabeth (Landgravine of Hesse-Homburg), Ernest (King of Hanover), Augustus (Duke of Sussex), Adolphus (Duke of Cambridge), Mary (Duchess of Gloucester), Sophia, Octavius, Alfred, and Amelia.

Who was the first monarch to ride in an automobile?

King Edward VII was an enthusiastic motorist and rode in a car for the first time in 1899.

How many of the 40 English/British/Commonwealth monarchs were buried outside England?

Five of them were buried outside England. Kings William I, Henry II, Richard I, and James II were buried in France and King George I was buried in Germany.

At which Commonwealth schools were Queen Elizabeth II's three sons educated?

Prince Charles, Prince of Wales, attended Timbertops School in Australia, Prince Andrew, Duke of York, attended Lakefield College in Canada, and Prince Edward, Earl of Wessex, attended Wanganui Collegiate School in New Zealand.

By what name was King Edward VIII known to his family before his accession to the throne?

His full name was Edward Albert Christian George Andrew Patrick David, and he was known by his family as David.

How might the British/Commonwealth royal family descend from King David?

Through the Exilarchs, or Princes of the Captivity, who were acknowledged descendants of the biblical hero king. Harun-al-Rashid, Caliph of Baghdad, it seems, sent Emperor Charlemagne one of these Jewish princes as an ambassador, a man called Makhir. Makhir stayed in the Frankish kingdom and founded a line of Exilarchs at Narbonne, from whom Queen Isabel, wife of King John (of Magna Carta fame), was in turn descended.

What disease did Queen Victoria pass on to some of her descendants?

Queen Victoria, through a mutant gene, was an originator and carrier of hemophilia, a blood disease suffered by males but transmitted by females. The queen passed it to the Tsarevich Alexei, heir to the Russian throne, through her daughter and granddaughter, the Empress Alexandra.

What is the *nom de brose* of the Prince of Wales?

When he signs his paintings, the Prince of Wales uses the name "Arthur G. Carrick." Arthur and George are among his Christian names and one of his titles is Earl of Carrick in Scotland.

What is "The Prince's Charities"?

"The Prince's Charities" is the collective name for the group of 20 charities founded personally by Prince Charles, Prince of Wales. He is patron or president of 18 of them and they are the largest multi-cause charitable enterprise in the United Kingdom. The areas of life covered by the charities, which operate in several Commonwealth countries, include opportunity and enterprise (especially for young people), education, health, the built environment, responsible business, the natural environment, and the arts.

Princes of Wales
- Prince Edward of Caernarvon, 1301–1307, later King Edward II
- Prince Edward, the Black Prince, 1343–1376
- Prince Richard of Bordeaux, 1376–1377, later King Richard II
- Henry of Monmouth, 1399–1413, later King Henry V
- Prince Edward of Westminster, 1454–1471
- Prince Edward of the Sanctuary, 1471–1483, later King Edward V
- Prince Edward of Middleham, 1483–1484
- Prince Arthur, 1489–1502
- Prince Henry, 1504–1509, later King Henry VIII
- Prince Henry Frederick of Stirling, 1610–1612
- Prince Charles, 1616–1625, later King Charles I
- Prince Charles, 1638–1649, later King Charles II
- Prince James Francis Edward, 1688–1688, 1701 (Jacobite status)
- Prince George, 1714–1727, later King George II
- Prince Frederick Lewis, 1729– 1751
- Prince George, 1751–1760, later King George III
- Prince George, 1762–1820, later King George IV
- Prince Albert Edward, 1841–1901, later King Edward VII
- Prince George, 1901–1910, later King George V
- Prince Edward, 1910–1936, later King Edward VIII and Duke of Windsor
- Prince Charles, 1958–present

Who was the first member of the British royal family to qualify as a pilot?

Prince Albert, later Duke of York and then King George VI, became a pilot in 1919. He also served in the fledgling Royal Air Force, the first member of the royal family to do so.

What is the George Cross?

The George Cross was created in 1940 by King George VI to honour civilians for their bravery, as the equivalent of the Victoria Cross for the Armed Forces. It was inspired by the bravery and sacrifice of the people during the blitz on London in the Battle of Britain.

Princesses of Wales

- Lady Joan of Kent, 1361–1385
- Lady Anne Neville, 1470–1472
- Princess Katharine of Aragon, 1501–1509
- Princess Caroline of Ansbach, 1714–1727
- Princess Augusta of Saxe-Gotha, 1736–1772
- Princess Caroline of Brunswick, 1795–1820
- Princess Alexandra of Denmark, 1863–1901
- Princess May of Teck, 1893–1910
- Lady Diana Spencer, 1981–1997
- Camilla Parker-Bowles, 2005–present (but uses secondary title of Duchess of Cornwall)

Where did Princess Elizabeth (Queen Elizabeth II) turn 21?

Princess Elizabeth reached the age of majority in Cape Town, South Africa, on April 23, 1947, during a royal tour of Africa.

Who was the only English monarch to be crowned king of France?

King Henry VI was crowned king of France in Notre Dame Cathedral in Paris at the age of 10 in 1431 after being crowned king of England in Westminster Abbey in 1429.

What was the name of the royal family's first corgi?

The first corgi was bought by the Duke of York (later King George VI) in 1933. It was a Pembrokeshire corgi called Dookie. Many of the corgis currently belonging to Queen Elizabeth II are direct descendants of Susan, a dog that she received as a present on her 18th birthday.

Who is the Duke of Lancaster?

Originally granted to John of Gaunt and his descendants in the male line, legally the title did not pass to the House of Tudor and succeeding monarchs, as Henry VII was descended from Gaunt through a female line. Nor can the title be held by the present queen as a female. However, since the Duchy itself was separated by Parliament from the other Crown lands and given to the sovereign as a source of revenue, the customary toast by Lancastrians today is "The Queen, Duke of Lancaster."

Quickies
Did you know ...
- that Queen Elizabeth II is a direct descendant of Genghis Khan?

Who named the Victoria Falls in Africa after Queen Victoria?

They were named in 1855 by Dr. David Livingstone of "Stanley and Livingstone" fame. The falls are bordered by Zambia and Zimbabwe and empty into the Zambezi River. They are neither the highest nor the widest falls but are believed to be the largest falls by volume of water flow in the world.

Consorts of English/Scottish/ British/Commonwealth Queens
- King Francois II of France (Mary, Queen of Scots)
- Prince Henry Stuart, Lord Darnley (Mary, Queen of Scots)
- James Hepburn, Earl of Bothwell (Mary, Queen of Scots)
- King Philip I of Spain (Queen Mary I)
- King William III (Queen Mary II)
- Prince George, The Duke of Cumberland (Queen Anne)
- Prince Albert, The Prince Consort (Queen Victoria)
- Prince Philip, The Duke of Edinburgh (Queen Elizabeth II)

Where is Lake Victoria in Africa?

Located at the junction of Uganda, Tanzania, and Kenya, Lake Victoria (Victoria Nyanza) is the source of the White Nile. Lake Victoria is the largest tropical lake in the world and one of the largest freshwater lakes.

What is Treetops?

It was the observation hotel built in a giant fig tree that overlooked a waterhole in Nyeri, Kenya, where Queen Elizabeth II was staying the night of February 5–6, 1952, when her father, King George VI, died in London and she became the queen.

How did Queen Victoria describe the audiences she gave to her famous prime minister William Gladstone?

Queen Victoria said of her regular sessions, "He speaks to me as if I were a public meeting." Leader of the Liberal Party, William Gladstone was a staunch monarchist but the queen preferred his equally loyal, but more diplomatic, rival, Benjamin Disraeli, leader of the Conservative Party, who also served as Queen Victoria's prime minister.

Quickies
Did you know ...
- that through her mother, Queen Elizabeth II is descended from Colonel Augustine Warner of Virginia, great-grandfather of George Washington, and is a second cousin, eight times removed, of the first American president?

Where was Prince Philip, Duke of Edinburgh, born?

A grandson of the king of Greece, he was born in his parents' home "Mon Repos" on the island of Corfu in Greece. After the fall of the Greek monarchy his family fled to the United Kingdom when he was a child, and he grew up in Britain, France, and Germany.

Who was the last Catholic monarch of Britain/the Commonwealth?

King James II, son of King Charles I and brother of King Charles II converted to Catholicism while he was Duke of York. He became king in

1685 and was overthrown by his Protestant nephew and son-in-law King William III in 1689.

On what significant anniversary was King George VI born?

Prince Albert, as King George VI was known until he became king, was born on December 14, 1895, the 34th anniversary of the death of his great grandfather, Prince Albert the prince consort, and he was named in memory of his ancestor.

How many children did King George V and Queen Mary have?

They had six children — five sons and one daughter — Princes Edward (King Edward VIII), Albert (King George VI), Henry (Duke

Dukes of York

- Prince Edmund of Langley, 1st Duke [1385–1402] (fifth son of King Edward III)
- Prince Edward, 2nd Duke [1402–1415] (elder son of Prince Edmund)
- Prince Richard, 3rd Duke [1415–1460] (nephew of 2nd Duke)
- Prince Edward, 4th Duke [1460–1461] and later King Edward IV
- Prince Richard, 5th Duke [1473–1483] (second son of King Edward IV)
- Prince Henry, 6th Duke [1494–1503] and later King Henry VIII (second son of King Henry VII)
- Prince Charles, 7th Duke [1605–1626] and later King Charles I (second son of King James I)
- Prince James, 8th Duke [1633–1685] and later King James II (second son of King Charles I)
- Prince Ernst August, 9th Duke [1716–1728] (brother of King George I)
- Prince Edward Augustus, 10th Duke [1760–1767] (brother of King George III)
- Prince Frederick, 11th Duke [1784–1827] (second son of King George III)
- Prince George, 12th Duke [1892–1910] and later King George V (second son of King Edward VII)
- Prince Albert, 13th Duke [1920–1936] and later King George VI (second son of King George V)
- Prince Andrew, 14th Duke [1986–present] (second son of Queen Elizabeth II)

of Gloucester), George (Duke of Kent) and John, and Princess Mary (Princess Royal).

Where is King Arthur's Round Table?

A table purported to be the celebrated Round Table is in the great hall of Winchester Castle. As its name suggests, the table has no head, implying that all who sat down at it were considered equal. The table is made of oak, is 18 feet across and nearly three inches thick, and weighs almost 1.25 tons.

Who proposed when Queen Victoria and Prince Albert became engaged?

Queen Victoria proposed to Prince Albert because she was the queen. The two were first cousins. He was 20 years old when they tied the knot and they had nine children together before he died at the age of 42, leaving the queen heartbroken. She lived for another 40 years but never remarried.

Quickies

Did you know ...

- that Queen Elizabeth II and Prince Philip, Duke of Edinburgh, are second cousins, once removed as well as wife and husband? They are both descended from King Christian IX of Denmark. They are also third cousins in descent from Queen Victoria.

Who was the first member of the royal family to enter the United States after the Revolution?

Prince Edward, later Duke of Kent and father of Queen Victoria, passed through the United States on his way to the West Indies in 1794. His brother Prince William, later King William IV, had been in the Thirteen Colonies that became the United States during the American Revolution and had been in North America after the Revolution but only in Canada and Newfoundland.

Who were united in an arranged medieval royal marriage that became one of history's great love matches?

King Edward I of England and his wife Queen Eleanor of Castile. Eleanor accompanied her husband when he went on a four year crusade to Palestine before becoming king, gave birth to their daughter at Acre, nursed the king when he was stabbed by a poisoned dagger, and accompanied him on many other military campaigns. Edward I's deep love for his wife is immortalized by the Eleanor Crosses he had erected at the twelve places her coffin rested for the night on its journey from Lincoln back to London in 1290.

Wives of King Henry VIII
- Catherine of Aragon
- Anne Boleyn
- Jane Seymour
- Catherine Howard
- Anne of Cleves
- Katherine Parr

What is the mystery of Queen Charlotte?

The question of whether the queen had very definite Negroid facial characteristics or not has been a topic of much discussion. The consort of King George III, Charlotte was directly descended in six different lines from Margarita de Castro y Sousa who belonged to a branch of the Portuguese Royal House thought to have black ancestry. Sir Alan Ramsay's official portraits of the queen appear to confirm the speculation. Copies of them were circulated by the abolitionists of the time. If this belief is true, then all of the Commonwealth monarchs since George III have been part black.

Who ordered Saxon royal pedigrees to be collected?

King Offa of Mercia, who died in 796, ordered family trees of the Saxon kings found and recorded for him.

Witches strove to prevent the arrival of which famous royal bride?

Princess Anne of Denmark. She set sail to Scotland in 1589 to marry King James VI but storms repeatedly drove her ship back to port. Finally her betrothed went to fetch his bride himself but the couple's subsequent return was also greatly impeded by storms. Three covens of witches, James found out, had been invoking the powers of evil to frustrate his intended marriage.

Quickies

Did you know ...

- that Queen Mary, wife of King George V, had been engaged to George V's elder brother Prince Albert Victor, Duke of Clarence, who died before the wedding could take place?

What native king almost united Ireland?

Countries (modern boundaries) of Birth of English/British/ Commonwealth Monarchs Since 1066	
England	27
France	6
Wales	3
Scotland	2
Germany	2
Netherlands	1

Brian Boru. Unfortunately he was killed in battle soon after achieving the union of the whole island with its warring kingdoms so his new realm did not last.

Which royal groom exclaimed "I am not well. Pray get me a glass of brandy" on seeing his bride for the first time?

George, Prince of Wales, later King George IV, when he met Princess Caroline of Brunswick. The couple were disastrously mismatched, produced only one daughter and quickly separated. As king, George IV failed in his attempt to divorce Queen Caroline but she died soon after his coronation from which he had excluded her.

Under which sovereign did Ireland become a kingdom?

King Henry VIII. The title was changed by the Crown of Ireland Act passed by the Irish Parliament in 1541. The king was granted a new title, King of Ireland, with the state renamed the Kingdom of Ireland.

The wily Elizabeth I never completely showed her hand. What did she say when asked her belief about the presence of Christ in the Most Holy Sacrament of the Altar?

The queen replied in an ambiguous little verse:

> 'Twas God the word that spake it.
> He took the Bread and brake it;
> And what the word did make it;
> That I believe and take it.

Which king assisted at his niece's bedding with the words, "So nephew, to your work! Hey Saint George for England!"?

The lusty King Charles II. His halloo was made at the official ceremony of putting the newlyweds to bed before the whole court, then a customary practice, following his niece Princess Mary's wedding to Prince William (William III "of Orange").

Which monarch did not know until he became king that his ancestor George III was the grandson not the son of George II?

King George V. Although a fine and intelligent monarch, much beloved by his peoples and with considerable common sense and understanding of human nature, that stood him well as king, he was not knowledgeable about family genealogy nor interested in academic study.

What were the famous last words of Charles II?

King Charles II was renowned for his wit and courtesy, and remained so to the end of his life. On his deathbed he said to his courtiers: "I am sorry gentlemen, to be such an unconscionable time a-dying."

How did King Charles II respond when a critic said of him, "He never said a foolish thing, and never did a wise one"?

The king replied that it was quite true, "For my words are my own, but my actions are my ministers."

a world
of royalty

Which 19th/20th century monarch was born a king?

King Alfonso XIII of Spain. He was born posthumously, six months following his father's death in 1885.

What was Emperor Maximilian I's unique scheme for European unity?

Quickies

Did you know ...

- that the word *mausoleum* comes from the great marble tomb King Mausolus of Caria, who died in 353 B.C., built for himself?

Maximilian I was Holy Roman Emperor and reasoned that if he also got himself elected pope then all Christendom would be united under a single head. The goal eluded him.

When was the Japanese Imperial Family founded?

It is believed that the family was founded in the year 660 B.C. The present emperor is directly descended from the first emperor, Jimmu, through more than 70 generations.

Which prince founded a republic?

William "the Silent," Prince of Orange, founded the Dutch Republic. More than two centuries later, the republic became a monarchy, with the House of Orange as its royal family.

Who was the first monarch to travel around the world?

David Kalakaua, king of Hawaii, who circumnavigated the globe in 1881, visiting Queen Victoria, the emperors of Austria and Japan, and other sovereigns on the way. In 1953–54, Queen Elizabeth II repeated the achievement on her first Commonwealth tour following her accession and became the first British/Commonwealth monarch to do so.

Who was the famous playwright Oscar Wilde named after?

He was named after King Oscar I of Sweden and Norway, who had been treated by Oscar Wilde's father, Sir William Wilde, a famous ear and eye surgeon, when the king was visiting London. Dr. Wilde asked, in lieu of payment for his services, permission to name his first son after the king.

Which two 20th century monarchs looked alike?

King George V and Tsar Nicholas II of Russia looked so much alike that they were virtually twins and when they were together people often could not tell them apart from a distance. The monarchs were first cousins through their mothers, Queen Alexandra and the Empress Marie, who were sisters and originally Danish before marrying the heirs to the British/Commonwealth and Russian thrones respectively.

Kings Encapsulated

- Henry VIII
  "If my head could win him a castle in France … it should not fail to go." — St. Thomas More
- Catherine de Medici
  "You may say she did harm to France — the marvel is she didn't do worse." — Henri IV
- Elizabeth I
  "Queen and huntress, chaste and fair." — Ben Johnson
- James I and VI
  "The wisest fool (i.e. jester) in Christendom." — Henri IV
- Louis XIV
  "His name is never uttered without respect." — Voltaire
- Peter I "the Great"
  "The outstanding epic figure of Russian history." — Florinsky
- George III
  "The Father of his people." — Mrs. Arbuthnot
- Louis XVIII
  "He was King everywhere, just as God is God everywhere." — Chateaubriand
- Victoria
  "That was a woman! One could do business with her!" — Bismarck
- Elizabeth, Consort of George VI
  "The most dangerous woman in Europe." — Hitler

What special honour are virtuous Catholic kings and queens eligible for from the pope?

The Golden Rose, an ornament fashioned of pure gold containing a tiny cup for musk and balsam, blessed by the pope on the fourth Sunday of Lent. Ironically, Henry VIII received it no less than three times. Henry VI was a recipient as were Mary I, Henrietta Maria (queen of Charles I), James III of Scotland, and Queen Mary Casimir (consort of King John III Sobieski). More modern Golden Roses have been sent to Isabella II of Spain, Princess Isabella the regent of Brazil, Queen Elizabeth of the Belgians, and Grand Duchess Charlotte of Luxemburg.

Which king is commemorated by a garden in Israel?

King Boris III of the Bulgarians has a garden dedicated to him at Migdal Ohr, Israel. The king is credited with having saved the lives of the entire Jewish community of Bulgaria, about 48,000 people, during the Second World War when Hitler demanded the deportation of the Bulgarian Jews to Germany. Soon after his courageous refusal to commit such an act of inhumanity, the king died suddenly and mysteriously, apparently poisoned on orders of the German dictator.

Is it true that Hitler hated monarchy because the Habsburgs favoured the Jews?

Yes. In *Mein Kampf* Hitler described the Habsburgs as "degenerate" and wrote that he was "repelled" by the mixture of races in Vienna, "and everywhere Jews, and more Jews." Joseph II, the 18th century Habsburg

Notorious Regicides

Killers of kings, called regicides, have always been looked on as the most horrendous criminals. Here are some regicides and their victims.

Macbeth	Duncan
William Ogle	Edward II
Edward IV, and Duke of Gloucester (Richard III)	Henry VI
King Richard III	Edward V
Friar Jacques Clement	Henri III
Queen Elizabeth I	Mary, Queen of Scots
François Ravaillac	Henri IV
John Bradshaw, Oliver Cromwell, Henry Ireton, Thomas Pride and 55 others	Charles I
Alexei Orlov	Peter III
Jacob Johan Anckarström	Gustavus III
380 members of the French Revolutionary Convention	Louis XVI and Marie Antoinette
Platon, Valerian, and Nicholas	Paul I
Nicholas Ryssakov	Alexander II the Tsar Liberator
Gaetano Bresci	Umberto I
Dragutin 'Apis' Dimitrejević	Alexander and Draga Obrenovich
Vladimir Lenin, Jacob Sverdlov	Nicholas II, Alexandra
Veličko cKerin and Mijo Kralj	Alexander I (Yugoslavia)
Mustafa Shukri Ashu	Abdullah II
Prince Faisal Ibn Musa'id	Faisal II

emperor, issued a Patent of Toleration giving freedom to the Jews and Francis Joseph, emperor of Austria and king of Hungary, 1848 to 1916, ended remaining restrictions on Jewish communities. Francis Joseph wrote: "The Jews are brave and patriotic men who happily risk their lives for Emperor and Fatherland."

Which monarch introduced Arabic numerals and algebra to Europe?

Frederick II, "Stupor Mundi," or "the Wonder of the World," Holy Roman Emperor, King of Sicily and Jerusalem.

What monarch was called "the peasants' king"?

Casimir III "the Great," king of Poland. Last of the Piast dynasty, Casimir III is credited with establishing a solid state structure for his kingdom. He carried out many reforms and founded Poland's first institution of higher learning, the Cracow Academy. In particular, the king tried to defend the peasants and protect them from exploitation by their lords. He also protected the Jews.

Which pope does Prince William of Wales descend from *legitimately*?

Pope Felix V. Prior to becoming a priest, Pope Felix V ruled as Amadeus V, Sovereign Duke of Savoy, married and had children, one of whom is William's forebear. Amadeus was not ordained until he was a widower.

What unusual Portuguese ancestry do Princes William and Harry of Wales possess?

Princes William and Harry of Wales are direct descendants of both Donna Ines de Castro of Portugal and Dom Diego Lopes Pacheco, who murdered her. Dom Diego was one of three Portuguese nobles who murdered Donna Ines, the secret second wife of Dom Pedro, heir to the Portuguese throne. When Dom Pedro succeeded to the throne as King Pedro "the Severe," he executed two of the three, but Dom Diego fled to England. William and Harry's father, Charles, Prince of Wales, is a descendant of Donna Ines and their late mother Diana, Princess of Wales, was a descendant of Dom Diego.

Where did the royal lines of the Anglo-Saxons, Teutons, Russians, Merovingians, Visigoths, and Lombards all originate?

All of these royal lines came from Scandinavia, descended from the sacral royalty of two great dynasties, the Skiöldungs and the Ynglings or "Peace Kings."

Which ancestor of Prince William of Wales founded the Order of the Golden Fleece?

Philip "the Good," Duke of Burgundy. He founded the order at Bruges (Belgium) in 1429. Inspired by the tale of Jason and the Argonauts' voyage to win the Golden Fleece from Greek mythology, the Order became associated through the Habsburgs with Spain and Austria. It is conferred today by King Juan Carlos I and by Archduke Otto, head of the house of Habsburg-Lorraine.

What is the Duke of Edinburgh's Award?

Prince Philip, Duke of Edinburgh, created The Duke of Edinburgh's Award program in 1956. It is dedicated to the personal, non-competitive development of young people from all backgrounds who challenge themselves to achieve certain set goals in a variety of activities. It has helped over six million young people worldwide through over 120 national Duke of Edinburgh's Award organizations in the Commonwealth and related organizations in other countries. The award was granted Royal Charter status in 2006 by Queen Elizabeth II in recognition of its work.

Quickies

Did you know ...

- that Sultan bin Salman bin Abdulaziz Al-Saud of Saudia Arabia was the first royal astronaut, going into space on the American space shuttle *Discovery* June 17–24, 1985?

Which American film star became a princess?

Grace Kelly, who married Prince Rainier III of Monaco in 1956, became

Imprisoned Monarchs and Their Jailers	
Richard I "the Lion Heart"	Leopold VI, Henry VI
John Balliol	Edward I
James I	Henry IV, Henry V, Henry VI
Richard II	Henry IV
Edward V	Richard III
François I	Charles V
Mary, Queen of Scots	Elizabeth I
Charles I	Oliver Cromwell
Sophie Dorothea	George I
Louis XVII	Antoine Simon
Napoleon I	George III, George IV
Napoleon III	Louis Philippe
Hsuan-t'ung Emperor (P'u Y'i)	Joseph Stalin, Mao Tse Tung

Princess Grace of Monaco. An actress who played a fictional princess in *The Swan*, she spent the rest of her life as the much loved consort of a real prince. She was killed in a car accident in 1982.

Where can you find some of the oldest royal genealogies?

They can be found in the Bible. The book of Genesis, in particular, presents extensive genealogies.

What was Kaiser Wilhelm II's reaction when told that King George V was changing his royal family name to Windsor?

Anti-German feeling in Great Britain and the Empire during the First World War forced King George V to change the royal family name from Saxe-Coburg-Gotha to Windsor. When informed that his cousin, King George V, had dropped the name of their mutual German grandfather Prince Albert, consort of Queen Victoria, the German kaiser casually remarked that he was off to the theatre to see the play by William Shakespeare, "The Merry Wives of Saxe-Coburg-Gotha."

> **Quickies**
> *Did you know ...*
> • that Tsar Nicholas II (Russia), his ally, and Kaiser Wilhelm II (Germany), his enemy, both were first cousins of King George V?

Which of the 28 statues of sovereigns on the magnificent German renaissance tomb of Emperor Maximilian I at Innsbruck is mythical?

The figure of Arthur, legendary hero and king of Britain, designed by Albrecht Dürer, is the sole unhistorical figure. His legend was so profoundly embedded in European culture and so real to Maximilian I's

Famous Royalists and Monarchs They Served	
Ivan Susanin	Michael (Russia)
James Graham, Marquess of Montrose	Charles I and Charles II
Jane Lane and Father John Huddleston	Charles II
John Graham, Viscount Dundee	James II
Flora Macdonald	Jacobite Charles III as Prince of Wales
Count Axel von Fersen, Chevalier De Rougeville	Marie Antoinette
Andreas Hofer	Francis I
Generals Miguel Miramó and Tomás Mejía	Maximilian (Mexico)

contemporaries that he was included as if he had been a true monarch and not a mythological one.

What one thing do the monarchs of Denmark, Norway, Sweden, and Spain share?

All are descendants of Albert "the Good," the prince consort and husband of Queen Victoria, and a major shaper of the practice of constitutional monarchy.

On July 14, 1789, the day that the Bastille in Paris fell, did King Louis XVI actually write in his diary "rien" (nothing), indicating that he was oblivious to the turmoil around him, as legend has it?

The word *rien* was not written in a personal diary, suggesting royal indifference. It was written in the king's hunting diary, indicating that the planned hunt for the day was cancelled because the king was engaged with the political crisis, not that he was indifferent to it.

What lost heir did the Greeks search for?

They were searching for a descendant of Emperor Constantine XI, ruler of Byzantium when the Turks seized the city in 1453. In modern times, after gaining independence, the Greeks wanted a king. They traced Constantine XI's family, the imperial house Paleologus, to Cornwall, and from there to Barbados, where the trail was lost. In the end, they had to take their king from another royal family, the Wittelsbachs in Germany.

Restorations of King and Queens	
Edward IV	England
Henry VI	England
John Casimir	Poland
Charles II	Great Britain, Ireland, and overseas provinces
Louis XVIII	France
Ferdinand VII	Spain
George II	Greece
Juan Carlos I	Spain

How did Emperor Franz Joseph II of Austria-Hungary describe the role of a monarch?

Speaking to an American journalist the emperor said, "I exist to protect my people from my ministers."

Which emperor had a family tree invented for him?

Basil I, Byzantine emperor, who was of Armenian peasant origin, had a magnificent but fictitious genealogy created by his descendants.

How is Charles, Prince of Wales, descended from Harold II, who was killed at the Battle of Hastings?

The prince is descended through the Russian ruling House of Rurik. Gytha, first

Quickies
Did you know ...
- that the 17th century philosopher-scientist Sir Isaac Newton, discoverer of the law of gravity, estimated the average length of royal reigns was 18 to 20 years?

wife of Vladimir II Monomakh, Grand Prince of Kiev, was the daughter of King Harold II by Edith "Swan Neck," and escaped to Germany after the Battle of Hastings in 1066.

What did Emperor Joseph II say when someone asked what he thought of the American Revolution?

"Sir," he said, "I am a royalist by trade!"

kings, queens, and dynasties

Monarchs of Canada

Royal House of Tudor

- King Henry VII, 1497–1509
- King Henry VIII, 1509–1547
- King Edward VI, 1547–1553
- Queen Mary I, 1553–1558
- and King Philip I, 1554–1558
- Queen Elizabeth I, 1558–1603

Royal House of Valois

- François I, 1534–1547
- Henri II, 1547–1559
- François II, 1559–1560
- Charles IX, 1560–1574
- Henri III, 1574–1589

Royal House of Stuart (and Orange)

- King James I, 1603–1625
- King Charles I, 1625–1649
- King Charles II, 1649–1685
- King James II, 1685–1689
- King William III, 1689–1702
- and Queen Mary II, 1689–1694
- Queen Anne, 1702–1714

Royal House of Bourbon

- King Henri IV, 1589–1610
- King Louis XIII, 1610–1643
- King Louis XIV, 1643–1715
- King Louis XV, 1715–1763

Royal House of Brunswick (or Hanover)

- King George I, 1714–1727
- King George II, 1727–1760
- King George III, 1760–1820
- King George IV, 1820–1830
- King William IV, 1830–1837
- Queen Victoria, 1837–1901

Royal House of Saxe-Coburg-Gotha

- King Edward VII, 1901–1910
- King George V, 1901–1917

Royal House of Windsor

- King George V, 1917–1936
- King Edward VIII, 1936
- King George VI, 1936–1952
- Queen Elizabeth II, 1952 –

Holy Monarchs and Princes

It is not easy to be a sovereign and a saint. Here are some who managed it.

St. Helena	Roman Empire
St. Oswald	Northumbria (England)
St. Edward "the Martyr"	East Anglia (England)
St. Stephen	Hungary, canonized 1083
St. Edward "the Confessor"	England, canonized 1161
St. Vladimir I "Apostle of the Russians and The Ruthenians"	Kiev (Russia)
St. Alexander Nevsky	Russia

St. Elizabeth "of Hungary"	Hungary and Thuringia (Germany)
St. Louis IX	France
St. Margaret	Scotland, canonized 1250
Ferdinand III "the Saint"	Castille and Leon (Spain), canonized 1671
Henry VI	Cause for his beatification begun by Cardinal Bourne 1938
Charles I "the Martyr"	Britain/Empire. Service for "the Day of the Martyrdom of the Blessed King Charles I" in *Book of Common Prayer*, 1662. Five English churches were named for him and others throughout the Commonwealth and U.S.
St. Elizabeth	Russia, canonized 1981
Nicholas II, Alexandra and other Romanovs	Russia, canonized 1981
Blessed Charles of Austria	Austria, Hungary, Bohemia, Slovenia, Croatia, Bosnia, Herzegovina, beatified 2004.

Monarchs of England

Saxons and Danes

- King Egbert, 802–839
- King Ethelwulf, 839–855
- King Ethelbald, 855–860
- King Ethelbert, 860–866
- King Ethelred I, 866–871
- King Alfred, 871–899
- King Edward I, 899–925
- King Athelstan, 925–939
- King Edmund I, 939–946

- King Edred, 946–955
- King Edwy, 955–959
- King Edgar I, 959–975
- King Edward II, 975–979
- King Ethelred II, 979–1013
- King Sweyn, 1013–1014
- King Ethelred II, 1014–1016
- King Edmund II, 1014–1016
- King Canute, 1016–1035
- King Harold I and King Hardicanute, 1035–1037
- King Harold I, 1037–1040
- King Hardicanute, 1040–1042
- King Edward III, 1042–1066
- King Harold II, 1066
- King Edgar II, 1066

Royal House of Normandy

- King William I, 1066–1087
- King William II, 1087–1100
- King Henry I, 1100–1135
- King Stephen, 1135–1154

Royal House of Plantagenet

- King Henry II, 1154–1189
- King Richard I, 1189–1199
- King John, 1199–1216
- King Henry III, 1216–1272
- King Edward I, 1272–1307
- King Edward II, 1307–1327
- King Edward III, 1327–1377
- King Richard II, 1377–1399

Royal House of Lancaster

- King Henry IV, 1399–1413
- King Henry V, 1413–1422
- King Henry VI, 1422–1461

Royal House of York

- King Edward IV, 1461–1470

Royal House of Lancaster

- King Henry VI, 1470–1471

Royal House of York

- King Edward IV, 1471–1483
- King Edward V, 1483
- King Richard III, 1483–1485

Royal York of Tudor

- King Henry VII, 1485–1509

see Monarchs of Canada for subsequent sovereigns

Famous Royal Mistresses

Sybil Corbet, Edith Sigulfson	Henry I
"Fair" Rosamund Clifford	Henry II
Alic Perrers	Edward III
Elizabeth (Jane) Shore	Edward IV
Françoise de Foix, Marie de Canaples	François I

Diane de Poitiers	Henri II
Louise de la Vallières, Athénaïs De Montespa	Louis XIV
Nell Gwy	Charles II
Catherine Sedley, Arabella Churchill	James II
Jeanne Poisson, Marquise de Pompadour, Jeanne Bécu, Countess Du Barry	Louis XV
Wilhelmina, Countess von Lichtenau	Friedrich Wilhelm II
Mary Anne Clarke	Frederick, Duke of York
Julie de St. Laurent	Edward, Duke of Kent
Dorothy Jordan	William IV
Lola Montez, Mairannina Florenzi	Ludwig I
Emily Langtry "the Jersey Lily," Alice Keppel	Edward VII

Favourites (not mistresses or lovers) of Royalty

Will Somers	Henry VIII
George Villiers (Duke of Buckingham)	James I and Charles I
Sarah Churchill, Abigail Masham	Anne
Princess de Lamballe, Princess of Polignac	Marie Antoinette
Heinrich Von der Tann	Ludwig I
Baron Stockmar, Baroness Lezhen	Victoria
Katharina Schratt	Francis Joseph

Monarchs of France

- King Charles I, 768–814
- King Louis I, 814–840
- King Lothaire, 840–843

Carolingians

- King Charles II, 843–877
- King Louis II, 877–879
- King Louis III, 879–882
- King Carloman II, 879–884
- King Charles, 885–888
- King Odo, 888–898
- King Charles III, 898–922
- King Robert I, 922–923
- King Raoul, 923–936
- King Louis IV, 936–954
- King Lothaire, 954–986
- King Louis V, 986–987

Royal House of Capet

- King Hugues Capet, 987–996
- King Robert II, 996–1031
- King Henri I, 1031–1060
- King Philippe I, 1060–1108
- King Louis VI, 1108–1137
- King Louis VII, 1137–1180
- King Philippe II, 1180–1223
- King Louis VIII, 1223–1226
- King Louis IX, 1226–1270
- King Philippe III, 1270–1285
- King Philippe IV, 1285–1314
- King Louis X, 1314–1316
- King Jean I, 1316
- King Philippe V, 1316–1322
- King Charles IV, 1322–1328

Royal House of Valois

- King Philippe VI, 1328–1350
- King Jean II, 1350–1364
- King Charles V, 1364–1380
- King Charles VI, 1380–1422
- King Charles VII, 1422–1461
- King Louis XI, 1461–1483
- King Charles VIII, 1483–1498
- King Louis XII, 1498–1515
- King Francois I, 1515–1547

see Monarchs of Canada for subsequent sovereigns until

- King Louis XV, 1715–1774
- King Louis XVI, 1774–1789

Illegitimate Offspring of Royalty

William I "the Conqueror"	Duke Robert of Normandy and Herleve (Arlotta)
Richard de Cornwall	Richard, King of the Romans and Jeanne de Valletort
Don Juan of Austria	Charles V and Barbara Blomberg
Henry Fitzroy, Duke of Richmond	Henry VIII and Elizabeth Blount
Don Juan of Austria	King Philip IV and Maria Calderón
Ruperta	Prince Rupert and Peg Hughes
Louis Auguste, Duke du Maine	Louis XIV and Athénaïs de Montespan
Louis Alexandre, Count de Toulouse	Louis XIV and Athénaïs de Montespan
James Scott, Duke of Monmouth	Charles II and Lucy Walters
James, Marshal Duke of Berwick	James II and Arabella Churchill

| Count Alexander Walewski | Napoleon I and Marie, Countess Walewska |
| Charles, Duke de Morny | Queen Hortense and Count de Flahaut |

Monarchs of Scotland

Royal House of Alpin

- King Kenneth I, 848–858
- King Donald I, 858–862
- King Constantine I, 862–877
- King Aed, 877–878
- King Giric, 878–889
- King Donald II, 889–900
- King Constantine II, 900–943
- King Malcolm I, 943–954
- King Indulf, 954–962
- King Dub, 962–967
- King Cuilem, 967–971
- King Kenneth II, 971–973
- King Amlaib, 973–977
- King Kenneth II, 977–995
- King Constantine III, 995–997
- King Kenneth III, 997–1005
- King Malcolm II, 1005–1034

Royal House of Dunkeld

- King Duncan I, 1034–1040
- King Macbeth, 1040–1057
- King Lulach, 1057–1058
- King Malcolm III, 1058–1093

- King Donald III, 1093–1097
- King Duncan II, 1094
- King Edgar, 1097–1107
- King Alexander I, 1107–1124
- King David I, 1124–1153
- King Malcolm IV, 1153–1165
- King William I, 1165–1214
- King Alexander II, 1214–1249
- King Alexander III, 1249–1286

Royal House of Fairhair

- Queen Margaret, 1286–1290

Interregnum

- 1290–1292

Royal House of Balliol

- King John de Balliol, 1292–1296

Interregnum

- 1296–1306

Royal House of Bruce

- King Robert I, 1306–1329
- King David II, 1329–1371

Royal House of Stewart/Stuart

- King Robert II, 1371–1390
- King Robert III, 1390–1406

- King James I, 1406–1437
- King James II, 1437–1460
- King James III, 1460–1488
- King James IV, 1488–1513
- King James V, 1513–1542
- Queen Mary I, 1542–1567
- King James VI, 1567–1625

see Monarchs of Canada for subsequent sovereigns

World Dynasties

For British/Commonwealth, Scottish, Irish, and French dynasties in detail see pages 178, 181, 184, and 188.

Alaungpaya	Burma
Alawid	Morroco
Al Khalifa	Bahrain
Al Sabah	Kuwait
Al Sanusi	Libya
Arsacid	Khurassan, Iran, Iraq
Ashanti	Ghana
Ascania	Anhalt
Assen	Bulgaria
Aviz	Portugal
Bagratid	Armenia, Georgia
Bernadotte	Sweden
Bourbon	Spain, Parma, Two Sicilies
Brabant	Hesse
Braganca	Portugal
Capet	France, Portugal
Carolingian	France, Netherlands, Germany, Italy

David	Israel, Judaea
Ghenis Khan	Mongolia, China, Iran, Crimea, Central Asia
Guelph	Hanover
Habsburg-Lorraine	Austria Hungary, Boehmia, Croatia, Slovenia, Mexico
Hashimite	Jordan, Iraq,
Herodian	Judaea
Hohenzollern	Germany, Romania
Hova	Madagascar
Inca	Ecuador, Peru, Chile
Iturbide	Mexico
Kamehameha	Hawaii
Mecklenburg	Mecklenburg
Merina	Madagascar
Merovingian	France
Ming	China
Moghul	India
Muhammad Ali	Egypt
Nassau	Luxemburg, Nassau
Nguye	Viet Nam
Nkosi-Dlamini	Swaziland
Oldenburg	Denmark, Greece, Norway
Orange-Nassau	Netherlands
Orleans-Braganza	Brazil
Osman	Turkey
Pahlavi	Iran
Palaeologus	Byzantium
Petrović-Nejoš	Montenegro
Ptolemy	Egypt
Rurik	Russia
Romanov	Russia
Saud	Saudi Arabia

Savoy	Italy
Saxe-Coburg-Gotha	Belgium
Seljuk	Iran, Iraq, Syria
Solomon	Ethiopia
Tui Kano-kupolu	Tonga
Vasa	Sweden
Visigoth	Greece, Italy, Gaul, Spain
Wettin	Saxony, Hanover, Brunswick, Bulgaria
Wittelsbach	Bavaria
Wurttemburg	Wurttemburg
Yamato	Japan
Yi	Korea
Zähringen	Baden
Zogu	Albania

High Kings of Ireland

- King Mael Sechnail mac Maele Ruanaid, 846–860
- King Aed Findliath, 861–876
- King Flann Sinna, 877–914
- King Niall Glundub, 915–917
- King Donnchad Donn, 918–942
- King Congolach Criogba, 943–954
- King Domnall Ua Neill, 955–978
- King Mael Sechnaill mac Domnaill, 979–1002
- King Brian Boruma, 1002–1014
- King Mael Sechnaill mac Domnaill, 1014–1022
- King Donnchad mac Briain, 1022–1064
- King Diarmail mac Mail na mBo, 1064–1072
- King Toirdelbach Ua Conchabar, 1072–1086
- King Domnaill Ua Lochlainn, 1086–1121
- King Muirehertach Ua Brain, ????–1119
- King Toirdelbach Ua Conchabair, ????–1156

- King Muirchertach Mac Lochlainn, 1156–1166
- King Ruaaidri Ua Conchabair, 1166–1186
- King Brian Ua Neill, 1258–1260
- King Edubard aa Briuis, 1315–1318

see Monarchs of England for subsequent sovereigns

Orders Founded by Sovereigns

Al Hussein	Abdullah I (Jordan)
Annunciation	Amadeus VI (Savoy; Italy)
Australia	Elizabeth II (Australia)
Bath	George I (Britain/Commonwealth)
Black Eagle	Frederick I (Prussia)
Black Eagle	Prince William of Wied (Albania)
Brilliant Star	Bagash Ben said (Zanzibar)
British Empire	George V (Britain/Commonwealth)
Cambodia	Norodom I (Cambodia)
Canada	Elizabeth II (Canada)
Carol I	Carol I (Romania)
Chrysanthemum	Meiji (Japan)
Crown of Rue	Frederick Augustus I (Saxony)
Crown of Wurttemberg	Wilhelm I (Wurttemberg)
Dignity	Moshoeshoe II (Lesotho)
Double Dragon	Empress Tsu-his (China)
Elephant	Christian I (Denmark)
Garter	Edward III (England)
Golden Fleece	Philip "the Good" (Burgundy; Spain; Head of House of Habsburg-Lorraine)
Golden Lion of the House of Nassau	William III (Luxembourg)
Golden Measure	Kwang Mu (Korea)

Holy Sepulchre of Jerusalem	Alexander VI (Papacy)
Holy Spirit	Henri III (France)
Icelandic Falcon	Christian X
Idris I	Idris I (Libya)
Indian Empire	Victoria (India)
Jamaica	Elizabeth II (Jamaica)
Kamehameha I	Kamehameha V (Hawaii)
Kalakaua I	Kalakaua I (Hawaii)
King Solomon's Seal	Yohannes IV (Ethiopia)
Legion of Honour	Napoleon I
Leopold	Leopold II (Belgium)
Ludwig	Ludwig I (Hesse)
Mahendra-Mala	Mahendra Bir Bikram Shah Diva (Nepal)
Maria Theresa	Maria Theresa (Austria)
Mexican Eagle	Maximilian I (Mexico)
Military Order of Christ	Denis (Portugal)
Million Elephants and White Parasol	Souka Seum (Laos)
Muhammad	Muhammad VI (Morocco)
National Hero	Elizabeth II (Jamaica)
Nichan Iftikhar	Ahmad I (Tunisia)
Nile	Hussein Kamil
Nishan-Imtiaz	Abdul Hamid II (Turkey)
Orchid Blossom	Kang Te (Manchukuo)
Order of Merit Principality of Liechtenstein	Francis (Liechtenstein)
Order of Merit	Radama II (Madagascar)
Order of Merit	Abdul Aziz (Saudi Arabia)
Pahlavi	Reza Shah (Iran)
Queen's Service Order of New Zealand	Elizabeth II (New Zealand)

Rose	Pedro I (Brazil)
Royal House of Chakri	Chulalongkorn Rama V (Thailand)
Royal Hungarian Order of St. Stephen	Maria Theresa (Hungary)
Royal Military Order of St. Henry	Henri Christophe (Haiti)
Royal Order of the Guelph	George IV (Hanover)
Royal Victorian Order	Victoria (for personal service)
Saints Cyril and Methodius	Ferdinand I (Bulgaria)
Saint Andrew	Peter I "the Great" (Russia)
Saint Charles	Charles III (Monaco)
St. Ferdinand	Ferdinand IV (Sicily)
St. George	Ernest Augustus (Hanover)
St. Hubert	Gerhard V (Bavaria)
St. Michael	Louis XI (France)
St. Maurice and St. Lazarus	Amadeus VIII (Savoy; Italy)
St. Michael and St. George	George III (Britain/Commonwealth)
Saint Olav	Oscar I (Norway)
Saint Peter	Danilo I (Montenegro)
St. Patrick	George III (Ireland)
Seraphim	Magnus I (Sweden)
Skanderbeg	Zog (Albania)
Sun	Emir Aman Ullah (Afghanistan)
The Crown	Abdul-Rahman (Malaysia)
The Crown	Alexander I (Yugoslavia)
The Redeemer	Otto I (Greece)
Thistle	James II (Scotland)
Two Rivers	Feisal Ghazi I (Iraq)
White Eagle	Vladislaw I (Poland)
White Eagle	Milan I (Serbia)
White Falcon	Ernest Augustus (Saxe-Weimar)
William	William I (Netherlands)

question
and feature list

The Nature of Monarchy

Royal Nomenclature

Monarchies in Action

Monarchy and the Military

Pomp and Pageantry

Royal Residences

Crown and Culture

Canada's Royal Ties

The Crown and the Commonwealth

A World of Royalty

Kings, Queens, and Dynasties